John Pendleton Kennedy

Mister Ambrose's Letters on the Rebellion

John Pendleton Kennedy

Mister Ambrose's Letters on the Rebellion

ISBN/EAN: 9783337417031

Printed in Europe, USA, Canada, Australia, Japan

Cover: Foto ©ninafisch / pixelio.de

More available books at **www.hansebooks.com**

Mr. Ambrose's Letters

on

The Rebellion.

BY

JOHN P. KENNEDY.

NEW YORK:
PUBLISHED BY HURD AND HOUGHTON.
BALTIMORE: JAMES S. WATERS.
1865.

Entered according to Act of Congress, in the year 1865, by
HURD AND HOUGHTON,
in the Clerk's Office of the District Court for the Southern District of
New York.

RIVERSIDE, CAMBRIDGE:
PRINTED BY H. O. HOUGHTON AND COMPANY.

A WORD TO THE READER.

THESE letters of Mr. Paul Ambrose were written at intervals, as their dates will show, from the close of the second year of the Civil War down to the restoration of peace after the surrender of Lee. They were addressed to the author's old friend, Mr. Seaton, of the "National Intelligencer," and, with the exception of the last, were published in that paper. The topics they bring into discussion are those suggested by the principles and incidents of the rebellion as these rose to view in the rapid transit of events. In the study of these topics the reader will not fail to remark how gradually and sharply the destined plot of this great drama was developed, from day to day, in the progress of what we might call the *ripening* of a wonderful revolution in the political and social character of the nation.

Mr. Ambrose has endeavored to explore the secret motives which impelled a class of politicians in the South, not without some effective coöperation from auxiliaries both in the North and West, to contrive the overthrow of the Union. He has also brought into review the most popular and authoritative assumptions of that political philosophy which may be said to be endemic in the South, and which has had such signal influence in swaying the mind of that region towards the unconscious but certain establishment of perpetual war between the States; for nothing is more fixed in the fate of nations than the impossibility of peace under conflicting sovereignties.

In the four years of desperate struggle that have gone by, the whole country has remarked how strangely each stroke of war smote the mind of the people with a new conception of the issue to which they were giving their strength. Each year brought a new phase to the conflict, every month unexpected change in its direction, new interpretation of its mysteries, stronger conviction of the power that shaped its course.

Now that the strife has come to an end, and we can look calmly over the wreck of the war and see how much the tempest of its wrath has destroyed, and how much it has regenerated and reformed, we are struck with amazement at the magnitude of the achievement: we acknowledge it to be far above all human premeditation; far beyond the reach of unassisted human agencies. We see in this consummation, the mysterious grandeur of an old Scriptural Prophecy or Proclamation of a Divine command; and we contemplate the end at which we have arrived with 'the awe and reverence due to the greatest and most memorable era, except one, that finds a record in human annals, — the Era of the Emancipation of four millions of Slaves, and the Extirpation of African slavery forever. The Curse of Ages has been lifted from two continents. Slavery has disappeared everywhere within our borders, and begins to-day to perish in Africa, to wither in Brazil, and all South America. The war has struck the blow that makes it henceforth incapable of life, beyond the present century, in any part of the world.

Everything that may serve to note the history of such an era, has a value that makes it worth preservation. It is chiefly on this score, that Mr. Ambrose has authorized the collection of these Letters in the present volume. But what had more force in bringing him to this conclusion, was the persuasion which led him to believe that, being written in the kindest spirit of old friendship, and, in great part, with a special view to the restoration of good will *South of the line*, they might do some service, if brought to the perusal of certain of our "Southern brethren" who have unwittingly, against all their antecedents, got strangely out of place in this quarrel. And it was added to this suggestion, that other of these brethren, of a more inveterate stamp, might, perhaps, experience a wholesome influence in turning over these pages, — if it were only for the opportunity it would furnish them for a review of their old teachings and traditional conceits touching government, which they had learned from the schools, and which had apparently so much to do in getting up this singularly miscalculated rebellion of theirs.

Now, to both of these classes of thinkers, these Letters — should they fail to convince those to whom they are tendered that they have fallen into error in regard to certain favorite dogmas — will, at least, offer a modest plea for the reconsideration of opinions which are now popularly claimed to be settled by the war, but which, I think, judicious persons would say, had much better be settled, if that be practicable, by argument and honest conviction. To bring this about would certainly be a point gained of inestimable value to the future peace and *cordial intent* of the country. Mere conquest is but a hollow peacemaker: it leaves the bitter root still in the ground. To pluck that out by the force of a true and manly judgment, instead of leaving it to die under the slow decay of time, will go far to turn our calamity into a blessing.

We have many points yet to settle, which will require all the wisdom and all the good temper on both sides, which the war has left us. In these pending and coming questions the South has a much nearer and more sensitive interest than the North. Let me give the men of that section a word of kind advice, in exhorting them to face their fortunes with an equal mind, to anticipate the predestined course of events, and to outrun the hopes of the country by ready and cheerful provision for the inevitable future. They have come to the threshold of a new nationality: let them cross it like a wise generation, with a brave confiding step, and they will live to rejoice in a new prosperity, more permanent and happier than the old.

JOHN P. KENNEDY.

BALTIMORE, *August* 1, 1865.

MR. AMBROSE'S LETTERS.

LETTER I.

JANUARY, 1863.

MY DEAR MR. SEATON: — This year, eighteen hundred and sixty-three, marks our entrance upon the third annual period of the civil war. The quarrel still rages with unabated fury. Indeed, as it grows older, it seems to become instinct with fiercer hatreds and to gather new vigor of resistance from its desperation. Is it not strange that such "a zeal to destroy" should so fire the heart of American citizens against the life of a nation whose birth and career have been the theme of more incessant, boastful, and extravagant panegyric than the affection of any people ever before heaped upon their country? Posterity will read the history of this commotion with an interest full of amazement at the intensity of the passion it has stirred in the hearts of its authors, and the utter insignificance of the provocation upon which it arose. They will distrust with natural wonder the narrative which informs them that large communities of intelligent people, as happy in their homes as a propitious Heaven and a beneficent Government could make them, peaceful and prosperous in the enjoyment of every blessing coveted by man, fondly addicted to self-gratulation for their well-earned eminence amongst nations, envied by the whole world for their freedom, conscious only of Government by its ever-present bounty; that they should turn upon the work of their own hands, and in a year of singular cheerfulness — a year of ovations, festivities, and pageants — should, all at once, convert their own Paradise into a Pandemonium, and fall to rending the magnificent structure of their liberties into fragments; that they should pursue this awful labor of demolition through two long years of such carnage and desolation as the world never saw before, and should, with still more bitter hate and eager ferocity, enter upon a third: that a thinking, shrewd, kind-hearted, Christian people should do this, with unremitting effort to render the obloquy and disgrace of the American name immortal! How shall after-ages study this terrible anomaly without a charitable doubt of its truth?

I know how painfully you meditate over this crisis, and I cannot but believe — nay, I am sure — that many of our old friends on the other side of the line are in full sympathy with us in deploring the madness that has brought our country into this unhappy distraction. If we could but reach them with an invocation to a calm review of those elements of discord which now separate us, I should be full of hope that the same wise spirit of counsel which won our confidence and love in past time, would bring us, as of old, into full accord, and that the kindly and powerful influence they were wont to exercise over the brotherhood, of which they and we were equally proud as citizens of our broad Republic, would be exerted within their own sphere, to stay the further rage of this tempest and open the path to that harmony and union which have been so causelessly disturbed.

With this intent and the indulgence of this hope, I address these letters to you, purposing, if haply the chances of the war should allow them to cross the line, to send them forth with a message of kind remembrance to old and cherished friends there, who I would fain believe have preserved their integrity and their reason unclouded by the passions which have hurried the multitudes around them into the dreadful vortex of the rebellion.

Your friend,   PAUL AMBROSE.

To W<small>M</small>. W. S<small>EATON</small>, E<small>SQUIRE</small>,
         Washington.

LETTER II.

SUDDEN CONVERSIONS.

JANUARY, 1863.

When a votary desires to make a sacrifice, he will find sticks enough under every hedge to kindle the fire. There is a Latin proverb to the same purport — "*Qui vult cœdere canem facile invenit fustem.*" My interpretation of this bit of experience is, that whenever we set our hearts upon a forbidden enterprise, an easy virtue will encounter no difficulty in the search for the means to get it on foot. Or, let me put it in another shape more germane to my present subject: Whenever it is necessary to support a bad or doubtful cause by an argument, he is but a sorry casuist who will have to go far to find one.

I am every day struck by the proof which the rebellion affords to the accuracy of this insight into the nature of the ordinary conscience of mankind. It is curious to note the facility with which, at this time, many of the most respectable minds of the country, even many eminent in public affairs, have permitted themselves to lapse into that fatal apostasy which, in a moment, has cast aside the honorable conservatism of their whole lives, and plunged them into that very maze of political error which they have always taught themselves and others to shun.

It is not long ago when it was almost the universal conviction of our most approved statesmen, both North and South, and still more that of the great multitude who take their opinions at second hand, that the doctrine of secession was a shallow invention of a few Quixotes in politics. In the days of Gen. Jackson it was denounced and derided as the blackest of treasons by the whole of that imperious party which, under his lead, swayed the public mind with absolute authority. When he said " the Union *must* be preserved," these words meant something more than a policy of conciliation; they were uttered as an angry threat against those who meditated disunion, and intimated that, if necessary, the Union should be preserved by the sword. The words were applauded by thousands and tens of thousands of those who to-day are crying out "this Union shall be destroyed." When he said, in strong and unequivocal phrase, that secession was treason, these same thousands reëchoed the sentiment with such earnest repetition as to plant it in the very heart of the country as an article of faith. The intuition of the masses in this conviction was sustained by the better informed judgment of the most eminent expounders of the Constitution, by the Courts, by Congress, and by the Cabinet, at that time illustrious for the great ability and experience of its members. It was not less sustained by the quiet support of nine-tenths of the educated men in every State, who, taking no share in the popular demonstrations of political action, gave their own healthful tone of thought to the social circles of their respective neighborhoods.

There were notable exceptions, it is true, to this common consent of opinion; many in South Carolina, where a threatened revolt had been staked upon the issue; some in other States, and more particularly in Eastern Virginia, where a peculiar system of traditionary dialectics had bred a class of hair-splitting *doctrinaires*, not less remarkable for the eccentricity of their dogmas than for the acuteness with which they maintained them. The philosophers of the Resolutions of '98 were few enough and grotesque enough, in the ordinary estimation of the country, to provoke a good-natured laugh at the perseverance with which they muddled their brains in the mystification of a problem that, in the common computation, had about as much practical value as that more celebrated scheme of Laputa, the extracting of sunbeams from cucumbers. But even the Resolutionists, for the most part, stood by Jackson, and turned their back upon the doctrine of secession.

Indeed, it may be affirmed, as an historical fact, that the whole South has, in different stages of our national career, at one time or another, repudiated this doctrine.

The present generation is but little aware, and many of the last generation of Southern statesmen now alive choose to forget, that there once was an occasion which called forth a great deal of notice of this pretension of the right of a State to secede from the Union, and that the prevailing sentiment of the South then branded it as a foul treason.

The Hartford Convention, after much preliminary announcement in the Legislatures of

New-England States, met in December 1814, to devise plans for the security and defence of those States in the war with Great Britain, and to adopt such measures of self-protection as were "not repugnant to their Federal obligations as members of the Union." A different purpose was suspected by their political enemies; and, whether justly or not, the popular belief of the South was, that, notwithstanding the restriction they had set upon their action, it was their design, in certain contingencies, to recommend the retirement of their States from the Union. The members of that Convention have vehemently denied this charge, but, so far as the South was concerned, utterly without effect. Every man, woman, and child of the South who was capable of receiving an impression from the topics of the day, heard the subject alluded to in conversation, or read of it in the papers, only as a scheme to dissolve the Union — a project of secession. It was at that time the word "secession" itself first became familiar as a term of our political vocabulary. Before that date Mr. Jefferson called it "scission;" and, by the by, pronounced it to be incompatible with any government. Whether, therefore, the Hartford Convention was slandered or not — as I believe it was — by this imputation, the general impression of its truth south of Mason and Dixon's line, brought up the opportunity for the expression of Southern opinion on the question of secession. Now, I am sure I am correct when I say that the imputed purpose of the Convention was denounced from one end of the Southern States to the other, with peculiar bitterness, as a purpose to commit a monstrous treason. They who remember the events of that day know that every leading man in those States, who made this supposed design of secession a theme for a speech from any forum; that the general current of popular opinion in educated society; the voice of the multitude which repeats the passwords of the day; and the whole flow of editorial comment in the most authentic presses, — all united in a common note of censure upon it as treason.

More recently, in 1850 and 1851, when South Carolina, in her vigilant outlook for an opportunity to strike another blow at the Union, thought she had found it in the admission of California, and had summoned the malcontents of the South to a new attempt at secession, every one remembers, how her favorite scheme of crushing out our nationality failed for want of coöperation from her sister States. The manly opposition of a loyal minority within her own borders, and, still more, the calm good sense of those to whom she appealed outside of her borders, defeated her charitable design. The people of Mississippi met in Convention and adjourned their deliberations with a sober resolution against the doctrine of a right of secession. Georgia discussed it, through the press and on the hustings, by her ablest exponents of constitutional law, and set her seal of condemnation upon it. It found no strength with which it was able to shake the faith of the people in their conviction of the right to be regarded as a *nation*. In that defeat there was nothing more to be admired than the instinctive recoil of the masses from the insidious teachings of ambitious politicians who sought to seduce them into this treason against the Government; nothing more significant of the common perception of the danger and disgrace of this principal of disunion than the dexterity with which some of the present oracles of secession then shirked the responsibility of appearing as its advocates.

In the Border States it had, at that date, no

foothold amongst men of any repute in society, except perhaps in the rare and scattered instances of a few super-subtle extremists on the theory of State rights. Even with them it was rather a speculation than a practical principle. Maryland might have had a handful of such men, but nobody heard of them. Kentucky and Missouri could boast of as few. Virginia, notwithstanding her passion for political metaphysics, though a little more demonstrative than the others, gave no further countenance to this heresy than the grandiloquence of a few of her country squires shed upon it when indulging their endemic proclivity towards the oracular at the monthly meetings of the county courts — the Solons of a great State, which they had seen, within their own days, dwindling down from a star of the first to one of a fifth magnitude in the firmament of the Union — a very natural experience to breed thoughts of discontent and separation.

In all this long period, from the date of the Constitution until that of the inauguration of this civil war, during which the fundamental ideas of our Government were acquiring solidity through that process of induration by which forms of polity become permanently established in the traditional respect of the people, *the nationality* of the Union was every day growing to be a more universally accepted fact. With the exception of a few sporadic instances of dissent, the mind of the country was settling down upon the conviction that the integrity of the Union was secured by the organic law, and could not lawfully be broken by any course of proceeding known to the Constitution or implied from the conditions under which it came into existence; in short, that nothing but rebellion and successful revolution could overthrow it. This conviction grew up in a state of peace which afforded leisure for calm and studious deliberation; a state of peace attended with such occasional perturbations as served to bring the question into prominent notice, and to invite a careful consideration of its terms and incidents, and yet free from that passion which is apt to cloud the judgment of the country. No national problem could be settled in circumstances more propitious to its true solution.

How does it happen, after such an experience with such a result, that, all at once, the year 1861 should find the question not only thrown into the wind, but the almost universal judgment of the country absolutely reversed, throughout a whole section of the South, embracing some eight or nine States and some four or five millions of citizens?

It would be very absurd to say that this change sprang out of a more thorough study of the history of the Government or a deeper insight into the philosophy of the Constitution. The year 1861 brought a tornado of violent excitements; men do not think with more careful deliberation in such a storm. It brought fierce ambitions into play, conspiracies, the clash of arms, the frenzy of party rage; these are not the companions of patient research or wise conclusions. In point of capacity the men of 1861 were not the superiors — I hope their *amour propre* will not be offended by my boldness — of Marshall or Story, of Madison or Hamilton, of Webster or Clay, of Spencer Roane or Lowndes, of Livingston or Jefferson, or even of Washington. How many more might I mention? Neither were these same men of 1861 wiser or more enlightened than they themselves were in 1851, when many of them took pains to teach their compatriots the fallacy as well as the danger of secession.

It is unpleasant to come to this conclusion, but there is no other left to us. We must look for this sudden abjuration of our ancient faith to causes which spring from less noble motives than conviction, and belong to a lower range of human action than that of honest judgment. We must submit to be disenchanted of the illusion that the many excellent men we were accustomed to admire, and among them so many of our cherished friends, were too staunch in their truth, and too courageous in their virtue, to be shaken by any popular tempest. Let us confess with sorrow that many — far too many to be thought of without a sigh for our country — had not the stamina for a time like this, and that they have either yielded to the spell of a popular excitement they had not the equanimity to withstand, or to the tyranny of a dictation they had not the manhood to brave. To one or the other of these influences they have surrendered the pride of their own intellectual eminence, their consistency, and their independence.

Yet, notwithstanding appearances to the contrary and the fact that many, from whom we hoped better things, had fallen off, I still believe that there is a host of true and patriotic men scattered through every State of the Southern Confederacy, who but bide their time to speak a potent word in support of that blessed old Union which the madness of our day has brought into jeopardy. I think you and I could name some of our old comrades, who will yet be heard sounding that clarion note of loyalty which the country has often heard in past time, when these very dangers now upon us were only looming in the distance. They are quiet now; many of them in voluntary exile, even in the bosom of the communities in which they dwell; silent and sorrowful, no doubt, and longing for the day when they may come forward to speak of peace. I would fain believe that many good men of this cast are held in reserve by Providence for that special service. They wait for the subsiding of the waters, when it may be safe to venture forth in quest of the olive-branch. With what full hearts and overflowing eyes will they be welcomed to our bosoms, if they bring us that sacred symbol! Let us wait and hope.

LETTER III.

SECESSION.

FEBRUARY, 1863.

It has been often said that the idea of restricting Government to a written constitution is a fallacy; that such a constitution is inevitably incapable of providing for the emergencies of national progress. The real constitution of a nation lies deeper than its visible ordinances, — in the character, habits, and customs of the people, which do not admit of a complete expression by instrument of writing. The written fundamental law provides only for what is foreseen, and is, therefore, but imperfect wisdom. What is not foreseen lies in the breast of the nation, to be taken care of, when it comes into view, by such mode of disposal as the case may require; either by process appointed for amendment, which is always slow and uncertain; or by gradual and imperceptible adoption, which is only the work of years; or by quick resort to such power as is at hand to meet an exigency which the nation recognizes as a necessity too urgent for delay. In one or the other of these modes a nation organizes itself and conforms its institutions to its needs. It crystallizes in the forms appropriate to its special quality. Thus all orderly government is manifested as a growth, and not merely as a formula.

We have something of a verification of this opinion in the changes which have already crept into our Constitution by the side-paths of usage, and in the constant tendency towards change which, if not accomplished, has yet given birth to many party contests to procure it. The practical alteration of the mode of electing the President is one example; the acquisition of territory, as in the purchase of Louisiana, is another; the recent enactment of legal tender and the suspension of *habeas corpus* are initiatory movements in the same direction, and may be regarded as a primary utterance of a necessity which in time may grow into established law. We may readily enumerate cases in which the Constitution — though now but seventy-four years old — has been modified, or at least settled by construction; and it is somewhat noticeable that in most of these expansions, if not invasions, of the letter, the strict constructionists have led the way. You and I can remember when the party now most active in urging the Government to make a railroad to California, was uncompromising in its denial of power to construct the Cumberland turnpike. Some of them were so conscientious as to refuse a vote for paving the Pennsylvania Avenue.

These scruples are obsolete now; not because the written law is changed, nor that it is discovered to admit of a new meaning, but simply because it does not meet the exigencies of national growth. A change in the organic law has been effected by construction — that is to say, by adding something to the Constitution, or taking something away from it, or otherwise interpreting its meaning.

I cannot find fault with this gradual adaptation of the fundamental law to the wants of the nation. In general, it is a healthful mode of change, and is ordinarily the natural expression of a necessity, — a tacit acknowledgment of the will of the nation that its institutions should be moulded to the public convenience, — and is apt to be a wiser process of amendment than that prescribed by law. It moves in the track of experience, and does not go beyond its requirements. Such amendments, indeed, are experiences, not experiments. We thus insensibly get out of the trammels of a written constitution, by building upon it, through a series of accretions, a traditional constitution which, in the course of a few centuries, will ripen into a solid organism exactly suited to the needs and instincts of the people.

The final good, however, is not attained without many alternations between failure and success, — the vibrations of the needle before it settles upon its true point. It is only reached through occasional struggles, turbulent conflicts sometimes, and sometimes great convulsions. The ordinary process of national development is, in the main, peaceable. A century of progress may go on without a war, but epochs emerge sooner or later when disputed demands come into the arena of debate and opposing ideas assert themselves in arms. No nation has ever reached its highest term of manifestation without a resort to the fierce arbitrament of the sword and many a field of blood.

This seems to be the normal law of human society, by which it is ordained that Governments shall arrive at their greatest capability through a career of strife and suffering. The sinews of nations are strengthened by conflict, and their virtues nourished by the discipline of pain and sorrow. We are at this day passing through one of these dreadful probations.

I think any man trained in the study of history might have predicted that at whatever period in our national career the doctrine of a constitutional right on the part of a State peaceably and at its own pleasure, to secede from the compact of the Union, was seriously asserted and attempted to be exercised by a party in the country or by one or more States, such an attempt would necessarily produce a conflict of arms. Whatever might be the question upon which the claimant should choose to institute this proceeding, — whether on commercial tariffs, on slavery, on domestic or foreign policy, or any mere project of ambition, it matters not what, — the enterprise would invoke the determined resistance of every man who cherished a regard for the nationality of the Union; and, if it could not be defeated by argument and persuasion, it would drive the parties into the collision of battle. If the advocates of the principle should succeed in that battle the old government would disappear, an entire new order of things would arise, and history would be furnished with one more example of disrupted empire and fragment communities settling into new forms or warring through ages of changeful disorder. If, on the other hand, they should be overthrown, the Constitution would come forth purified and renovated by the ordeal, and would strike with deeper root into the soil of the national faith and take a more sturdy growth in the attachment of the people. I think these might have been the predictions of any learned student of the prevailing sentiment of the American people, without waiting for the insight afforded him by the sad realities of the present day.

For myself, I do not hesitate to affirm that I think this doctrine of a right of secession so intrinsically mischievous, so incompatible with any national progress, and so destructive of all rational hope of peace or happiness, that if it really had any place in our system, it should be the first duty of this generation to get rid of it at any cost; that, in this earnest effort of combined States to plant it amongst the acknowledged rights of the members of the Union, it is worth all the sacrifice of this war, however long me. may be protracted, worth all the tribulation it has brought or may bring us, to free our posterity from a heresy so full of evil to us and to them.

Notwithstanding the vehemence with which this right is now asserted, the question, I am happy to believe, is not yet removed from the domain of argument which may be addressed, with some hope of patient consideration, to many honest minds in the South, to whom the disappointments of defeat or, at least, the delay of success, may have brought a calmer judgment and a more complacent temper. It is in that hope I expand the limits of this letter.

No one, I believe, has ever claimed Secession to be one of the rights acknowledged by the Constitution to reside in the States. The second section of the sixth article of the Constitution would seem to infer exactly the reverse. Its advocates generally claim it as a *reserved* or, more properly, an *implied* right, resulting from, what they assert to be, the original Sovereignty of the States. They say, that the States, being sovereign when they entered into the Union, and being the creators of the Union, necessarily retain all their original sovereignty — which they affirm to be inalienable by any compact — to be exercised whenever they think proper:

that, in fact, they are bound by the laws of the Union only as long as they choose to remain in it.

I have two objections to make to this statement. The first relates to the character and nature of the sovereignty claimed by the States, which I shall notice more at large in a future letter, affirming, for the present, that the States possess no such sovereignty as is claimed for them. The second objection I make is — that, supposing a State to possess every attribute of sovereignty compatible with our system of government and to the fullest extent asserted by the defenders of the doctrine, it may, quite as effectively as an individual person, enter into a social or political compact and bind itself to the conditions and duties of that compact, even to the complete and perpetual surrender of its separate existence as an independent corporation.

This is precisely what the original States did, so far as they acted, as States, in forming the Constitution. But, combined with this State action in forming the Constitution, there was another party to the compact, more powerful than the States — the people of all the States, who designated themselves as " the people of the United States " — the nation — who were the acknowledged repositories of all power, both over the States and over the National Government, and who, in that name, declared the supreme law by which both the National and State Governments were to be controlled in the due administration of the system they proposed to the country. In short, they, the people, created the United States and made them emphatically one nation, 'with supreme powers within the orbit assigned to it.

The question is simply reduced to this: Do the United States constitute A NATION, or do they represent an agglomerate of nations, bound together by a temporary bond of a texture so feeble that any one may lawfully put an end to the combination whenever it may find a motive to do so? Was it the intention of the States and the people really to construct a temporary alliance of separate nations, dependent for its duration upon a tenure so frail as the possible and probable discontent of a dominant party in any one of the associated nations?

The answer to this question will lead us directly to a consideration of what we must suppose to be the common-sense view which the founders of the Government took of the enterprise they had in hand, — I mean to the estimate they made, whilst they were engaged in moulding the Constitution, of the object they intended to accomplish. This is an *a priori* view of their purpose, and avoids all debate upon those subtleties of interpretation which, at a later day, ingenious logicians have invented to prove a right of secession.

What did the authors of the Constitution intend to establish, when they met together to frame a Constitution for the Government of the United States?

I waive all reference to that record of historical facts, which is now extant, to prove that the controlling majority of the Convention discussed the question, and maturely decided that their purpose was to erect a nation out of Confederate States, which nation should possess every function of supremacy necessary to preserve its own existence; and that to establish and secure such supremacy the several States should surrender, or, in more appropriate phrase, should be denied every attribute of sovereignty that could interfere with or impede the free and full exercise of the national sovereignty it was their design to create, and equally their declared intention to render perpetual.

I waive all reference to this record, and, for the present, look only to what must have been the common-sense view which these clear-sighted men took of the task committed to them. Did they deem it expedient or wise to invest, either by grant or implication, the States then existing, or which in future time might be organized, with what is now claimed as the right of secession?

In responding to this inquiry it is only necessary to reflect upon some of the most prominent and obvious consequences which follow the practical application of this right. We shall then be able to determine how far these are compatible with the design of the Constitution, as this is apparent in its text.

It is not a strained conclusion to assume that the architects of the structure intended to make a self-preserving and not a self-destroying Union; that they proposed a system which should protect the vital interests of the country, not expose them to unnecessary peril; a system that would work through coming ages and promote the prosperity of many generations.

Looking at their projected labors in this light, I proceed to remark upon the incidents which the most ordinary foresight would discover as the probable attendants upon the exercise of a right of secession, and which our late experiment of it has brought into view as actual impending dangers.

1. The retirement of any State from the Union, even in the mildest mode of such a proceeding, could not but be accounted a most disastrous calamity, full of peril not only to the domestic peace of the country, but also to its foreign relations.

An act of secession by the smallest State in the Union would make that State, according to the theory, an independent government. In that character it would have a right to form alliances with foreign powers, to place itself under their protection; even to unite itself as a dependency to the most formidable enemy of the States it had left, and thus give to such an enemy a foothold on the soil, with all the advantages he could desire for invasion, — the very danger which it was a prime object of the Union to avert. It would be in the power of the least of the States, in this category, to disturb the regulation of the national commerce, by the adoption of an adverse system of trade, by discriminating duties, by restricted privileges of navigation, and other devices of annoyance.

It would furnish a refuge to fugitives from justice, and, what is worse in the computation of ills, according to the ethics which have lately grown almost into a religion in some portions of our country, to fugitives from servitude. It is easy to conceive how very inconvenient such a neighbor might become to the general welfare of the nation by a thousand forms of vexation open to the practice of the most inconsiderable State in such a relation.

How much more significant and aggravated would be these irritations in the case of the secession of a large central State like that of Pennsylvania! Can we believe that the framers of our National Government contemplated with complacency the possible contingency of a large and powerful Commonwealth, lying in the very bosom of the Union, erecting itself into an independent government, and assuming a character that might, in any event, authorize it to embarrass the communication between the North and South; to exact duties upon every transit of merchandise; to demand passports from every traveller, or totally to interdict both and compel the severed fragments of the nation to seek their intercourse with each other by a long *détour* around her borders? Can we persuade ourselves that the men of 1787 had in their thoughts the foundation of a Union that should be subject to such contingencies as these?

2. Secession not only endangers the national welfare by planting a foreign nation within the circle of the Confederacy, but it absolutely paralyzes the Government by depriving it of the capacity to perform its most necessary functions.

The Government is authorized and, by its needs, required to contract debts and to pledge the faith of the whole nation for their payment: Secession rends it asunder and disables it from performing this pledge.

The Government makes treaties: Secession repudiates or impairs them.

The Government builds forts, creates armies and navies, founds arsenals, establishes mints, post-offices, hospitals: Secession seizes, appropriates, or destroys all these within the reach of its arm.

The Government acquires territory, holds public lands, and erects States: Secession confiscates these possessions and applies them to its own profit.

The history of Florida affords a striking

illustration on this point. That territory was originally purchased by the United States at the cost of five millions of dollars. Some fifty, or perhaps a hundred millions more were expended in its defence. It was purchased on considerations purely national, as essential to the commercial and military advantage of the country. It contains about thirty millions acres of available land, which, by the purchase, became a public domain. Emigrants from other States went there and were allowed to settle on this domain upon payment of a small amount per acre for the fee. In the year 1845 there had emigrated into this territory a population which, added to the settlers already there, amounted to something less than forty thousand white persons, who had become the owners of perhaps some two or three millions of acres. In this year, 1845, these persons very earnestly desired the privilege of being erected into a State, and to that end petitioned the Government of the United States to confer upon them this greatly desired boon. At that date the high tariff of 1842 was in full operation; the question of slavery was as rife, as active, and as virulent in its agitation of the country as it has ever been since; in short, every Southern grief, as interpreted in the inflamed politics of our day, was as poignant at that time as it was in 1860. Notwithstanding these motives " to heap curses upon the Union," which some of the most authoritative teachers of Southern rights were then urging upon their disciples, the people of Florida, with their eyes open to all the " iniquities" they now impute to the National Government, prayed for admission, and they were kindly received and welcomed as a loyal addition to the fellowship of States.

After a brief existence of fifteen years, during which the Government was known to them only by the profusion of its bounties, upon some pretence of convenience — for they had none of oppression — they avail themselves of this right of secession to enable them to retire from the Union. By this act they not only claim to deprive the people of the United States of the whole benefit of the considerations which originally induced the purchase of this territory from Spain, as a national necessity — the great forts upon the coast, the naval depots, the supply of ship-timber, the light-houses and guides to navigation, and the means of protecting the commerce of the country — but they also assume a right to the eminent domain of all the public lands and to appropriate them according to their own pleasure. The white population of Florida to-day is about double what it was in 1845, something less than eighty thousand; and if we suppose the public lands they have seized and sequestered by this exercise of the lawful right of secession to be twenty millions of acres, they would be able to divide amongst the present white men, women, and children of Florida something more than two hundred and fifty acres of land apiece, which would represent the *legitimate* profit of a right which, it is asserted, the founders of the Government of the United States, deliberately and in the full exercise of their wisdom, reserved to the people of the States.

Certainly, we might very reasonably presume that, if the framers of the Government contemplated such a possibility as the case of Florida presents, now in actual existence, they would have ordained, as an indispensable enactment of the Constitution, that no territory acquired by the nation should ever be lifted up into the dangerous eminence of a State; that, indeed, the " old Thirteen " alone should limit the circle of sovereignties armed with this power of spoliation; that no other portion of the national domain should be permitted to hatch its cockatrice brood of serpent States to sting the parent which nursed them in its bosom.

3. The Constitution declares that "no State shall, without the consent of Congress, enter into any agreement or compact with another State." Secession, as its first step, annuls this law and seeks auxiliary alliance from its neighbors.

Nothing would be so impracticable, and therefore nothing so improbable, in the development of this doctrine of secession, as the attempt of a single State of the Union to set up for itself an independent nationality, to be maintained without the aid and concurrence of other States. The geographical relations of certain groups of States, into which the Union is divided by climate and production and by similarity of institution, present, very distinctly to our notice, characteristic affinities which create, both socially and politically, a more intimate connection between the members of these several groups than is observable in the larger and more important circle of the Union as defined by the Constitution. The Planting States form one of these groups; the Western

States another: so of the Middle States, and, further north, the New England. They are all associated in one grand and beneficent political bond; but, in these minor and natural divisions, they are allied by sympathies and sentiments which grow out of proximity of position and that identification of pursuit and interest which the conditions of their social life impress upon them.

When any State, therefore, should meditate the purpose of withdrawing from the Union, in the exercise of this asserted right, it would naturally, and indeed we may say it would necessarily, as an indispensable auxiliary to its purpose, seek the alliance of the States which stand in kindred relation with itself, and would use all the means at its command to enlist them in its cause.

So apparent is this necessity to persuade or seduce other States whose prejudices or sympathies may be wrought upon to concur in the work of disruption, that it may be regarded as the most flagrant mischief that attends the assertion of the right to secede. It brings up before us that enormous wrong, — the most deadly which can be inflicted on any State, — the secret plotting of eager agents of discontent to inflame the heart of peaceful communities with imaginary griefs, and rouse them to the temper of an assault against the existence of the nation. It shocks us by the perception of a danger of disintegration which, once commenced, may go on until the whole political fabric is crumbled into fragments.

In the events which have plunged the nation into its present state of distress we have notable exemplification of this incident of secession. The discontents of South Carolina — the first State which inaugurated the civil war — were notoriously peculiar to that Commonwealth. They had existed for thirty years, and were greatly exasperated by — if indeed they did not owe their birth to — the quarrel of 1832, when the pride of the State was humbled by the peremptory measures taken by the National Administration. At that period her claim to a right of secession was, as I have shown in a former letter, not only bluntly repelled by the Government, but equally repudiated by every State in the Union, and Carolina was forced to submit not less by the threat of *coercion* by President Jackson, than by the rebuke of the States to which she had appealed for coöperation. Her mortified pride made her from that era the inveterate enemy of the Union. In the act of secession of December, 1860, she only accomplished the long-harbored design for which she had been waiting with ill-concealed impatience ever since the arrow had pierced her side.

Yet, notwithstanding the rash boast with which she entered into this fatal measure — that she would plunge into the maelstrom of secession alone, irrespective of coöperation from any other State — no one believes that she would have assayed the experiment if she had not ascertained beforehand that she would be supported by the auxiliaries which immediately afterwards hastened to her aid. There is abundant proof in this concerted movement — if we had it not from other sources — that, long before and in preparation for this event, a conspiracy had been formed to seduce, cajole, or compel other States into complicity with a plot which she had contrived and set in motion for the redress of her own griefs.

The whole country knows with what signal and almost indignant reproof several of the States now in rebellion rejected the first overtures to join in this enterprise; how emphatically the people of Virginia, Tennessee, North

Carolina, Georgia, Arkansas, and others expressed their disapprobation of the petulant and boastful treason of South Carolina. And yet the country now sees these very States subdued to the service of the conspiracy by the intrigues and domineering importunity of the political agents who had cast their fortunes in this venture.

It is therefore, that I say the worst evil, attendant upon the practical assertion of this pretended right of secession, exists in the fact that an imperious necessity forces the agents of the plot to the device of infusing their own discontent into the minds of neighbor communities, and of seeking, by unlawful solicitation and sinister arts, to spread the circle of the conspiracy over other States. Thus, the letter and the theory of the Constitution are violated and set at nought by overtures and by compact and agreement with other States, which, whether secret or open, are equally offensive and repugnant to the obligation that every State assumes on entering into the Union.

4. Secession very distinctly assails and destroys the personal rights conferred by the Constitution upon the people of every State in the Union.

Being a citizen of the United States I am entitled to all the privileges of that citizenship in every State. In other words, no State within the compass of the Union, as created by the Constitution, can treat me as an alien. This I take to be the meaning of that clause which guarantees to the citizens of each State "all privileges and immunities of citizens in the several States."

Secession in a moment rescinds and ignores this right. He who holds a patent for an invention, or copyright of a book, loses it throughout the seceded States. He who possesses property in such a State, or an expectation of an inheritance in it, may be deprived of it by seizure and confiscation or by escheat: if he be a creditor he may be forbidden to sue for or collect his debt. In all these cases the American citizen, who is secured by the Constitution against any interference with these rights, becomes dependent on the comity merely of the seceding State for their acknowledgment. Whatever may be the policy of such a State in regard to this acknowledgment — whether it be swayed by temperate and just counsels or by the angry passions which are most likely to predominate in the separation — it is obvious that the citizen of the nation loses every personal as well as public right, which the forethought of his ancestors had conferred upon him, in so much of his native land as is cut off by the scission, and is left entirely at the mercy of the State for such favor as its Government, exasperated it may be by his obtuseness in not assenting to the teaching of secession, may be disposed to grant.

5. The right to secede from the Union implies a right to expel from the Union. If one can withdraw from many, many may withdraw from one. If the Union may become inconvenient or disagreeable to one, one may become disagreeble to the Union. If one, for that reason, may retire, why may not the others for that reason expel? The Constitution makes no regulation for either case; and if the logic of secession be sound — that the State sovereignty may be resumed on a motive of discontent, and is then at liberty to adopt its own "mode and measures of redress" — the logic is equally sound that infers in favor of a majority of State sovereigns, being discontented with one, the same liberty to adopt *their* own mode and measure of redress. These rights — if there be any right at all to break up the

compact of Union — are correlatives. Can any champion of these transcendent State-rights distinguish between the lawfulness of these two proceedings of secession and expulsion? Both have the same foundation, if either have any, in that sovereign " will and pleasure " which secessionists affirm every State retains *in petto* as a reserved prerogative.

Now, we may fancy with what a fiery burst of insulted majesty one of these hot-headed States which have been so arrogant in their claim of a right of secession — South Carolina, for example — would have resented a proposition of expulsion suggested to the Council of the Union by any other State as the peaceful process allowed by the Constitution to get rid of her as a troublesome sister. Imagine the flare-up in the Old Dominion against the insolence of such a proceeding applied to her. What conclaves should we not have, what a flurry of political conventions, what a buzz and hum in every village, what indignant protests against usurped power from sophisters of the State-rights academy, what refined distinctions and discriminations from the abstraction-mongers, and what instant threat of war, seizure of Gosport Navy-Yard, of Harper's Ferry, of forts and arsenals, and all the other violences and menaces which burgeon from the stock of Southern temper! What! claim a right to drive a sovereign State out of the Union made by our fathers; to deprive us of our inestimable privileges as members of the Great Republic, whose birth was consecrated by the blood of heroes from every State and shed upon a hundred fields; to strip us of our proud prerogative of American citizenship; to derange or destroy our commerce; to deprive us of our rights in the common domain, won by the united strength and valor of all the States; to take away from us the protection of the common defence, our share in the benefits of the common treasure, and to cast us upon the wide world a dwarfed and dishonored people, a prey to the power and domination of any enemy who may find it his interest to subdue us; and then to insult our intelligence by telling us that your right to inflict this injury and disgrace upon us is a right reserved to you by the founders of our Union!!!

What a volume of such rhetoric as this would be poured out at every cross-road hustings in the whole country!

Repulsive as the assertion of such a claim as

this would be to the cherished traditional idea of national unity and to the common perception of the duty of securing to every State its rights in the Union, in which the people of the United States have been educated, it is not more repulsive than that parallel and correlative claim of a State to retire from this connection at its own pleasure. Of the two, the latter is the least tolerable in a fair, statesmanlike estimate of its incongruity with the general welfare of the nation; for, whilst the first is the most improbable of all contingencies in the progress of government, and would never even be thought of but under such provocation as, in the nature of things, must be so excessive, persistent, and enormous as to be, in common experience, impossible; the latter, as our recent history proves, would be an ever-present danger from its adaptation to the use of political faction and from its quality to captivate the multitude by its flattery of State pride.

To an earnest and thoughtful reflection on the attributes of our Union and the dangers to which it is exposed, it must occur that all that can be urged against the expulsion of a State, may be with equal force, and with deeper conviction of the necessity of impressing it upon the popular mind, be urged against the secession of a State. The arguments touching the right are the same; the mischief to be averted is incomparably the greater in the case of secession.

I might enlarge this enumeration of the anomalies which become apparent in the contrast between the manifest design which the authors of the Constitution had in view, and the equally manifest incidents which belong to the practical application of this pretended right of secession. But it is only necessary to glance at those which I have arranged under these five divisions, to perceive that the antagonism is so positive and so destructive of the scheme of the Union which occupied the thoughts of the legislators, that to impute to them such an obstruction, as a premeditated contrivance, is to charge them with the folly of constructing a machine which, by its inherent disregard of mechanical laws, was incapable of performing its most necessary and important functions — a machine which must soon jar itself out of all possibility of action and tumble to pieces by the strain of its own friction. We should lose all respect for the memory of such bungling workmen, as this theory would compel us to regard those great and good statesmen who have, for seventy years, been consecrated in our affections as the wisest and best of the founders of States.

So far, in the consideration of this question of secession, I have confined my view to the difficulties which the doctrine presents as an impediment to the administration of the Government in conformity with the obvious design of the Constitution. In the next letter I shall discuss it more briefly under another aspect.

LETTER IV.

SECESSION.

March, 1863.

If we could accord to the philosophy of the Southern school the merit of even a plausible theory, in its inculcation of the right of secession, and could admit that this right secured a principle which a State might, in some possible emergency, find it useful to bring into practice for its own advantage, and that, contemplating the rare occurrence of such a possibility, the framers of the Constitution did really intend to give it a place in their scheme, as a latent power to be awakened into activity only as a substitute for revolution, we should find ourselves arrested at that point by the remarkable failure of the Constitution to provide for its own execution; and, in the total absence of all regulation upon this subject, we should be obliged to conclude either that this feature of the scheme was abandoned, or that, in some moment of drowsy forgetfulness, those notoriously vigilant and astute gentlemen whom we are accustomed to laud as the sages of our golden age — Washington, Hamilton, Franklin, and the rest — had withdrawn from their watch and left their otherwise consummate work not only unfinished but actually too imperfect to admit of the first step towards the demonstration of this element, which, it is said, they intended to incorporate into the structure. On this matter of secession they preserved a silence so profound, and so extraordinary — if they had any consciousness of its existence — as to make it the most obscure and helpless of antiquarian studies to determine, at this day, whether a solitary man of that era ever heard the idea of secession broached, or ever dreamed of it himself. Nothing so difficult now as to tell when it was first thought of, who originated it, and where it is to be found.

Looking to the portentous magnitude of this power, to the embarrassments it would produce, and the contingencies it would create, it is inconceivable that law-makers of the most ordinary sagacity could recognize it as an existing principle in their scheme of government, without devoting a chapter to its definition and to the necessary provision for its consequences. They would have devised ordinances to meet every category into which an act of secession would have thrown the country. They would have pointed out the *modus operandi*, — the assembling perhaps of a National Convention, the manner of announcement of the proposed withdrawal, and the arrangement of its conditions. They would have made a rule for the division of public property, the payment of debts, the modification of treaties, the protection of private rights, the disposal of territory, and the numerous other matters affecting the public peace and safety, which this destructive process would call into urgent notice.

To make secession what it is claimed to be, a *peaceable* proceeding, would require a code of legislation of the highest wisdom. Without such legislation its attempt could be nothing else than a turbulent, headlong rush into a *melée* of fierce political strife.

Now, we are to suppose that, with all these necessities and direful consequences in view, our fathers consented in silence to this malignant power; that they delivered to their posterity the great work confided to their labor — the creation of an Union designed to be as perfect and as nearly perpetual as human wisdom could make it — with the seeds of this mortal disease planted in its heart, planted with their knowledge and approval; that they made no provision to mitigate its virulence or assuage the pain of its stroke; did not even name it, but left it a silent and lurking poison in the inmost depths of the Constitution, to destroy the life of the nation whenever occasion might awaken it into activity. We are to believe this, and then exalt our fathers amongst the benefactors of mankind, as the first founders of a State who ever had the sagacity to provide a power for the early and swift destruction of their own work, and to leave that power under the simple guidance of its own unregulated discretion, or, as present events interpret it, its own blind passion.

This conclusion is the more revolting to us, when we reflect, in the light of events now disturbing the country, by what dishonest means a State may be driven to practice this method of separation; how much it is at the hazard of faction; how the proceeding may be procured by a forced vote against the will of the people; how it may be stimulated by the mad impulses of a day, in some access of that capricious rage to which the passions of the multitude are so easily excited by popular leaders. This step once taken, the natural drift of events soon makes it irrevocable. No day of calmer judgment, no future repentance of a generation weeping over the crime of their ancestors, may haply find the juncture suitable to restoration. Or if that season to retrieve the error come, how mournfully may it illustrate, by its delay, the dreadful catastrophe of a plunge into an abyss from which the return is only through an ocean of blood and years of sorrow!

Turning aside from these considerations, which seem to be sufficiently cogent of themselves to settle the question, I propose to devote this letter to a few remarks upon what I regard the total unsoundness of the argument by which the advocates of the right of secession generally undertake to maintain it. They are accustomed to affirm that it legitimately results from the theory of the original or antecedent sovereignty of the States; that the States, when they entered into the compact of Union, reserved all the rights of absolute sovereignty, to be resumed by them, whenever they, in their own judgment of the necessity, might think proper to do so. They go further than this, and, refining upon the nature of sovereignty, they say that this right to resume did not require any assertion as a reserved power, but necessarily resulted from the inherent and inalienable quality of sovereignty; that it is of no avail in the argument to inquire whether the founders of the Union had or had not a conception of secession, the right to withdraw from the compact was still there in virtue of the original sovereignty, and could not be given away even by the State itself. It was something of " a higher law," a kind of divine right, far above the Constitution and Union; a right which lay in *nubibus*, or — in language more suitable to its high pretension — in the empyrean, until it was wanted here on earth. This is the transcendental extreme of the Southern philosophy on the subject. The Seceding States have acted on this theory. Some of them simply *repealed* the declaration of their assent to the ratification of the Constitution; repealed, as Mr. Everett has well stated it, " an historical fact," — implying, by that act, that what was once a fact of past time is no longer a fact; they repealed the fact that, in the year 1789, Virginia agreed to come into the Union on the terms proposed, — an incident no more repealable than the surrender of Yorktown. The act of ratification was a deed, not a law; it was an acknowledgment of fealty to the United States, which neither party conceived was an act subject to any modification or repeal by any future legislature or convention. Since that day the higher law has been discovered, and has been brought down from its cloudy abode — *deus ex machina* — to throw our whole continent into confusion.

I need not say, after what I have written in my previous letter, that I totally dissent from every item in this summary of the doctrine of secession; but, for the present, I pretermit all objection to the theory it proposes, and proceed to notice the condition in which it leaves the question.

Suppose it be a sound principle that this right results from the original sovereignty of the State, and that no compact, however solemn, can bind a State to the renunciation or circumscription of its sovereign attributes longer than it is its own continuous will to be bound; or suppose that those States, in forming the Union, actually reserved this right, as the prerogative of their antecedent sovereignty, these admissions would bring us to the recognition of an anomalous diversity in the composition of the Union, which has never hitherto been perceived, and which would, if it really existed, become the source of endless quarrel. The right of secession, on this foundation, would be limited to those States only which can establish a claim to an original or preëxisting sovereignty. The Union would be divided into States having the right, and States not having the right — one portion of the Confederacy elevated in rank and majesty above the other. Those having the right would be the "old Thirteen," with the addition of the State of Texas, which came into the Union bringing with it the attributes of a previously existing sovereignty.

The Union now consists — speaking of it as it was at the commencement of the rebellion — of thirty-four States. Of these, twenty-one have been created by act of Congress; and amongst these twenty-one, Texas alone had an anterior existence as a sovereign power. Twenty of the States, therefore, are, as limited sovereignties, the mere creatures of the National Government.

Can it be claimed for these twenty States, that they hold a reserved right to *resume* their sovereignty and to retire from the Union as independent nations? Clearly, *resumption* is not the word applicable to them. How resume what they never had, — absolute and independent sovereignty? So there is another distinction that cannot be got rid of, — States in the Union that may resume, and States that may not resume. These new States, if they do anything in this way, must *seize* what was never given to them, — must *usurp* a prerogative they never had, in order to bring them to an equal dignity with the old States, or elevate them to the rank of Texas. That is the absurd dilemma of secession. Many of those States are formed on territory purchased by the National Government for the benefit of the nation; all of them on territory either purchased or ceded for the advancement of the common welfare. If they lapse from their present condition by abandoning their privileges in the Union, one would naturally say they lapsed back into their original predicament. That is precisely what the old States claim by their secession. The new States would fall back into Territories, the old ones into Sovereignties. And thus we have another distinction between the States, logically resulting from the theory of secession. The idea that the new States could lapse into something greater than their original condition is a solecism that, in a less grave argument, would be called "a bull." The Territories were not *given away* to the people who inhabit them, but *organized* for the use and advantage of the Union. They had no antecedent sovereignty whatever. They were clothed with no power but that which was necessary to make them loyal members of the American Union. The most absurd thought that could be imputed to Congress, when it gave them political existence, is, that in elevating them to the rank of States, it was giving them a power to destroy the Union, and to aggrandize themselves at the expense of all the other States. It is simply preposterous to say that the Constitution contemplated any such consequence when it authorized Congress to create new States. If such a consequence could, in any contingency, lawfully result from this power, no greater folly could be ascribed to the people of the United States than that of authorizing any Territory to be erected into a State. It would be a cheap way of despoiling the Union of its most valued possessions.

At one time the Government intimated a wish to purchase Cuba for one hundred millions of money. What possible inducement could persuade an American statesman to desire such an acquisition, if the acknowledged, lawful consequence of such a purchase could, in any event, authorize the inhabitants of that island, after they were organized as a State of the Union, — which would have immediately followed, — to withdraw from the compact and assume an absolute sovereign dominion over that rich possession, appropriate its land to their own use, and deprive the nation of all the advantage it designed by the purchase? Yet such is the claim made by the right of secession, and such not only the possibility, but, judging from our recent experience in the case of Florida and Louisiana, the imminent probability of the assertion of this right. Once let the people of Cuba into the secret of our "verdant simplicity" on this point, and we open to them the perception of an easy and profitable device by which they may obtain one hundred millions of our money and still secure Cuba to their own disposal and control.

This is a *reductio ad absurdum*, and ought to be conclusive to any sound judgment, that the right of secession cannot be predicated, at least in the case of the new States, — I mean the States created by act of Congress. Now, I think it is good argument to say, that if there be no right of secession in the new States, it does not exist in the old. Our system was designed to be homogeneous. We detect no discrimination between the States in their constitutional description. They are all designated by the same investiture of rights and duties; literally equal in all attributes and relations. The distinction between new and old is simply chronological. The authority to make additions to the Union is given in few words, without qualification. "New States may be admitted by Congress into this Union." That is all the Constitution utters on the subject.

It could not have escaped the authors of this clause that the new States would, in process of time, grow up to great influence and importance in the system. They probably foresaw that these States might eventually come to constitute, in numbers and wealth, the most powerful portion of the Union; for they had even then large territories in their view which were beginning to germinate in the development of political organization. New acquisitions of territory were probably not beyond the forecast of many members of the Convention.

They were also convinced that no disparity of rights between old and new States would ever be recognized or tolerated.

Now, the new States — those to be formed out of the public domain — having no pretence to a right of secession deduced from original sovereignty, could only obtain it by express grant. Such a grant no one has ventured to contend is found in the Constitution. We may fairly argue that if the framers of the Constitution believed the old States had this right by implication, they would have also conferred it upon the new by grant; that they did not so confer it on the latter, is proof that they did not believe in its existence in the former. The conferring of it upon either would have been to recognize what I have shown to be, in the old States a right to perpetrate a most flagrant injury upon the country, and, in the new, a right to aggravate the crime of breaking up the Union by adding to it the inducement to plunder the public treasury by the trick of seizing the public domain; — even, in a supposable case like that of Cuba, to convert a large appropriation for a purchase into a gratuity without an equivalent. Doubtless the answer to this insinuation would be, that the honor of the States which boast of their chivalry may be safely trusted that no such wrong would be inflicted. That might have been a plausible answer years ago. But look at Florida now. Look at every seceding State that holds any portion of the public domain. Look at the seizure of the mint, — the early and swift confiscation of all Government property, — as the first steps in the rebellion. We shall have a settlement of all these, perhaps, at the Greek Kalends!

I have but one more point to notice in my reference to the special grounds upon which the secessionists defend their doctrine, and with that I shall finish this letter and dismiss the subject.

The whole argument in favor of secession is founded on a *petitio principii* which I hold to be totally inadmissible. The common statement of that argument is, that the Union is but a confederacy of sovereign States; merely a complex *league*, in which each member retains all the sovereignty of an independent nation; that the Federal Government is nothing more than an agency created by these States for the convenience of performing certain functions for their benefit. From this statement, the deduction seems to be universally accepted by the secessionists, and even too carelessly allowed by their opponents, that the Union being a league, any member of it has a right to withdraw whenever it chooses to do so. They concede that if the United States were a *Nation*, in the proper sense of that term, they could not do this. A *League*, they say, presents a different case. A member may withdraw from a league.

Now, I do not mean to spend any time in controverting the basis on which this proposition rests, — the affirmation, namely, that the Union is simply a league, or that it was created only by the States. That notion has been abundantly refuted by abler pens than mine. But I deny the deduction drawn from this basis. If this were true, in point of fact, I think it a great mistake to affirm that the member of a League of sovereign States has any right to retire from the association at its own pleasure.

A league between States is a compact more solemn and more binding than an ordinary treaty between nations. It has all the characteristics and responsibilities of a treaty; but it has something more. It involves the delicate relations of a *government* within the orbit assigned to it; invites and necessitates the adoption of a course of action and policy which pledges a common faith to the due observance of numerous obligations indispensable to the daily discharge of its functions. It is constantly contracting engagements to which every member of the league is bound, and which, being for the benefit of the whole, cannot be repudiated by one without inflicting a wrong — sometimes a vital wrong — upon the rest.

In respect to a common treaty between two nations, it may be said, in a loose sense, that either party has a right to declare that the treaty has been violated by the other; but the other has an equal right to deny the infraction. If they cannot accommodate matters, the only resort for a settlement of the difference is to war. To retire from a treaty is to give a lawful cause for war. There is no such thing known as a peaceable right to secede from a treaty, unless the treaty contains an express stipulation to that effect. Such a right never results from the single fact of the absolute sovereignty of the parties.

What foundation, then, is there for the assertion that, in a league, this sovereignty of the parties gives each this right?

The old Confederation which existed before the present Constitution, was strictly a league of States. It did not pretend to be a nation. Yet nothing was more abhorrent to the ideas of the men who formed, and acted under, that Confederation, than this notion of a right existing in any member to secede from it, or in any manner to alter its terms but by the unanimous consent of all the members. The nature and force of the Confederate obligations on this point are well defined by Luther Martin in his address to the Legislature of Maryland, on his return from the Convention which formed the Constitution.

Speaking of the old Confederation, he says:

" That in forming our original Federal Government every member of that Government, that is, each State, expressly consented to it; that it is a part of the compact made and entered into, in the most solemn manner, *that there should be no dissolution or alteration of that Federal Government without the consent of every State, the members of and parties to the original compact;* that, therefore, no alteration could be made by the consent of a part of these States, or by the consent of the inhabitants of a part of these States, which could either release the States so consenting from the obligation they are under to the other States, or which could in any manner become obligatory upon those States that should not ratify such alterations."

This argument was used by Mr. Martin in support of his opposition to the mode proposed by the Convention for the ratification of the Constitution by the concurrence of seven States; and, being used simply in the way of argument, was an appeal to the received opinion of that day in reference to the old Confederation,—an opinion which, apart from his own high authority, was clearly a correct one. Now, it must be observed that the Articles of Confederation are as silent as the Constitution on the subject of secession. Mr. Martin's argument is a deduction from the nature of the compact or treaty of Confederation; that, although the States were recognized in that compact as absolute sovereignties, they could not *dissolve* or *alter* the Government without the unanimous consent of the members in the league. Where was the right of secession if this view is a sound one? The whole of Mr. Martin's address, which is an elaborate discussion on the principles of the Constitution, is worthy of study in reference to this question. He was a harsh critic upon the labors of the Convention; saw many defects in the Constitution which time has proved to be imaginary; made many prophecies of its malign influence upon the country which have never been fulfilled; complained of its *nationality* as pregnant with mischief to the States, and even went so far as to say, " we considered the system proposed to be the most complete, most abject system of slavery that the wit of man ever devised under the pretence of forming a Government of free States;" yet, with all these evil portents looming upon his disturbed vision, it never occurred to him that there was lodged in this system a power which could in a moment shiver it into atoms, and thus dissipate all these apprehensions of the terrible bondage to which he fancied these "Free States" were doomed. Indeed, it is impossible to read that address without perceiving, on every page, that the idea of secession never entered into his thoughts, and had never been entertained by the men of that day. It would have at once dispelled all his fears and answered half the objections he so anxiously urged against the work of his compatriots.

The student of our history will find many testimonies in the records of our initiatory era, in addition to this of Mr. Martin, which will be equally conclusive to convince him that no man who had any part in the fabrication of the Constitution, nor any portion of the public who anxiously watched the progress of that work, ever intimated an idea that a right to withdraw from the Union existed either by inference or grant as a privilege left to or conferred upon the respective States. Upon that point the silence was universal and pregnant with meaning. It is very evident that generation regarded the compact as designed to be perpetual. They would not even agree, as may be seen in Mr. Madison's letter to a member of the New York Convention, to allow a State to make a conditional ratification, by way of experimental probation of the Constitution, before a final acceptance of it. It was to be perpetual; they must take it so, or not at all, is the import of his direction.

We have no difficulty in perceiving that the founders interpreted the ratification as an irrevocable surrender by each State of all the power required to be surrendered for the common benefit. And, as the Government was the compound result of State action and popular action, the surrender of power by the State was an act which was confirmed and rendered doubly irrevocable by the concurrent vote of the people of the whole of the States, who came in as a third party, binding themselves and their States to the compact, through their several State Conventions. Out of this joint action between States and people grew A NATION, in which was skilfully and beautifully combined two sovereignties, — the one the complement of the other, — a national sovereignty supreme in the national sphere; a State sovereignty supreme in the State sphere; neither clashing with the other, but both together making up the whole sum of sovereignty which is essential to a complete nation. The States were clean shorn of every vestige of sovereignty in the circle allotted to the National Government; and the National Government was, in like manner, shorn of every vestige of sovereignty in the circle appropriated to the State government. They were complements to each other; and the National Government has just as much right to abrogate the State power and release itself from its obligations to the States, as the States have to abrogate the national power and release themselves from their obligations to the nation.

This view of the mutual relations between the two authorities distinctly defines national rights and State rights, which are equally clear, equally sacred, and equally guarded against encroachment from each other.

It has not been my purpose to comment at large upon these principles in our Constitution, or to gather up the numerous demonstrations of them which our early history affords. My chief object in this and the former letter was to show that the States and people of the United States have contracted obligations, by the compact of the Constitution, which are totally irreconcilable with the asserted right of secession; that, with the impediment of this right, the harmonious and even the most indispensable performance of the functions of our Government would become impossible, and that the foundation of the right, as asserted by its advocates, has no support in the views entertained by the founders, or in the institutes of national law.

LETTER V.

REVOLUTION.

October, 1863.

Notwithstanding the pretence set up by the movers of this great disorder in the country, their scheme is nothing more nor less than an attempt to subvert the Government by a revolution. It suited their purpose to claim it as the exercise of a peaceful right of secession.

We perceive many obvious motives of policy to suggest to them this expedient. If they could persuade the country that the States were merely asserting a right which belonged to them as members of the Union, they would, to the extent of that persuasion, be able to confront the Government with the charge of denying to them their admitted privileges under the Constitution. Whether wise or not in seceding from the Union, would be a question upon which people might differ; but the right would not be controverted. If they could impress the world with this opinion, then it would follow that to resist them would be adjudged by the world to be a simple and inexcusable act of aggression. The Government would be regarded as the assailant, and they would be the injured party. They might, with this advantage, appeal to the sympathies of mankind as a people oppressed by unlawful force, and assume the part of patriots contending for their dearest rights. They would present themselves to the tribunal of public judgment as legitimate, independent States, having a claim, by the law of nations, to immediate recognition by all other Powers; not States struggling in the throes of revolution to make themselves free, but States free in their antecedent life, and now, by virtue of the common fundamental law, free from all alliance with their late associates, self-controlling and in full organization as nations from the moment they severed their connection with the Union. In such an aspect of their case, the law which controls the policy of nations, on the question of recognizing a people who revolt against their rulers, would have no application. The question would not arise, " Are these people able to detach themselves from the Government that ruled them, and to maintain their attempted nationality by their own strength ?"

but it would be, with all the outside world, " What right have we to refuse to acknowledge the existence of a body politic which, by the organic law of the Confederacy to which it was once attached, has become an independent nation, through the appointed form of a declaration of its own will to be so?" The admission of this principle annuls the whole law of treason in respect to the retiring State. It is no longer under the jurisdiction of the common Government. Its people owe no allegiance to that Government; they have, in a moment, become aliens. If war be made upon them, it is a war of established belligerents; they are alien enemies to each other; and the party that begins the war must find its justification in the ordinary code of nations applicable to the disputes between foreign Powers. The mere act of separation, being in pursuance of an actual right, is no just cause for war. The retiring party has committed no offence. All he asks is, " Let us alone." This was the convenient theory upon which the fomenters of this commotion ostensibly commenced their operations. According to this theory there could be no rebellion, and, of course, no revolution. The Governments of the States and of the Union were only developing their future in the due process of the normal law of their construction; falling to pieces, it is true, but falling to pieces in pursuance of the design and in the manner prescribed by the authors of the Constitution.

This is the *rationale* of their action, as explained in the official expositions of the government set up in the revolting States, and which is urged, with eager reiteration, upon the cabinets of Europe. As yet they have met no acknowledgment of their claim. The cabinets persist in regarding the war as rebellion and its aim revolution. Foreign Powers, therefore, we may infer, do not accept the doctrine of secession. It is true, some foreign statesmen, who are well-wishers to the downfall of the great American Republic, and who delight to encourage any plot which may compass so happy an end, give, now and then, a stimulating hint of their favorable conviction on this point; but no nation has yet been so hardy as to make it a ground for interference in our quarrel. They, one and all, subject the question of intervention to the test afforded by national law and usage as applied to the case of revolting fractions of a State.

There being no right of secession, as I have demonstrated in my last two letters, the whole movement to sever the Union is simply an enterprise of revolution. No proclamation of a more lawful foundation for it, no pretension of a different purpose contemplated by its leaders, no protestation of innocence of treasonable design, by the thousands who have taken up arms, or of the multitudes of men and women who afford material aid and comfort to the movement, or encourage it by their sympathy, can alter its nature. The object aimed at is revolution, and the means are rebellion. The champions of the cause are rebels. If the rebellion be without such justification as the moral law sanctions, then it is one of the blackest of crimes; the rebels are traitors, and they justly incur the penalty of treason. If, on the other hand, there be such justification for an effort to subvert the Government as is recognized in the moral code of the most enlightened nations, the rebellion is without guilt, and the rebel, notwithstanding the offence which the law may impute to him, is untainted by the crime of a traitor. It is the Government, in that case, that betrays, and the citizen lawfully resists.

This is a brief summary or outline of the ethics of rebellion, as expounded by the most liberal jurists of this age, and as universally accepted in our country. There is no right we are less disposed to deny than that of revolution. It is an instinct of American society to sympathize with the revolt of a people against their rulers. We are perhaps too apt to do so from an *a priori* presumption that every government oppresses somebody, and that people never revolt without good cause. There is a popular attraction in the idea of fighting for "our rights," — a phrase often more alluring to a love of adventure than susceptible of definition. I have no doubt that the Southern armies are filled by the influence of this sentiment. Rash and thoughtless young men, who have never paused a moment to inquire into the merits to the cause, have rushed into rebellion simply because it was rebellion. Men of riper years have thrown themselves into it, with that traditionary idea that revolution itself is a glorious incident, and that it is heroic to sustain it. I think this trait of our national character will disclose the secret of much of that enthusiasm which has spread over the South and brought the rebellion into favor with many worthy men who, to this day, are unable to give an intelligible account of the motives which seduced them into the conflict. I think it will explain the phenomena of epauletted bishops and priests in jackboots, deserting their vineyards to swagger in the camp. I think it will satisfactorily solve the riddle of the remarkable virulence with which the women on that side scream out their joy at every wound that is inflicted upon their country. Rebellion has become the fashion in that gentle world, and, like another fashion there, is utterly heedless of the uncleanness into which it dips its skirts.

Passing by these illusions or mere stimulants of temper which have driven so many to the compromise of their loyalty, I propose to explore the real motives, as far as they are attainable, that have led men of influence and capacity to attempt so bold and desperate an enterprise as the overthrow of the Government.

In looking for these motives, we should expect to find either, on the one side, some oppressive feature in our Constitution or some inveterate and incurable evil in its administration ; or, on the other, some mistaken conception of injury resulting from Government, some intolerable anomaly of social life only imagined curable by separation; or, in the absence of inducements as honest as these, some depravity of personal ambition daring enough to meditate the destruction of the State in order to compass its ends. I remark, in clearing the way for this inquiry, that the first man is yet to be found, North or South, who, in the way of excuse for rebellion, has alleged that he has suffered wrong from a solitary act of this Government. No man has been so bold as to affirm that there is a single statute in the national code, a single decree of the Executive; that there is any treaty, or any judicial decision of the national judicature, which has ever given offence to a Southern citizen or afforded any fair ground of complaint to a Southern State, at the date at which this rebellion was inaugurated. It does not abate the truth of this assertion to say that there have been, in the seventy years' experience of the Union, various questions of policy broached and determined, upon which political parties have differed; that laws have been passed, treaties made and Executive proceedings adopted, which roused the opposition of parties, both in the North and the

South. These are but the regular and anticipated incidents of all popular government, and, indeed, manifest the healthful freedom of opinion by which alone all good governments are preserved. These divisions of opinion were general, pervading the whole country, and distinctive of no section. What I mean to affirm is, that no legislation ever transcended the natural and proper limits prescribed to the legitimate action of the Government in determining and shaping the public policy; that nothing has been done but in accordance with the power given by the Constitution, and what the Constitution contemplated as the appropriate office of legislation. There were tariffs enacted, there were laws prohibiting and laws allowing slavery in the Territories, internal improvement and national-bank laws, upon all of which there were various dissenting opinions and frequent political conflict; but all this legislation was founded upon precedent established in the earliest age of the Government and continued to the latest; and, what is of some significance in this view, these laws were passed during the long period in which the Government was mainly directed under the control of Southern votes. No sensible statesman could find in such legislation an honest ground for rebellion. They were acts of administration, changeable at the will of the people. It would be as absurd as wicked to make them the pretext for overthrowing the Government.

Indeed we have the testimony of the rebels themselves that the structure of the Government afforded them no cause of complaint; for they immediately adopted the same Constitution, with some few modifications, as the framework of their own Confederacy. Amongst these modifications they did not even incorporate that which might be regarded as descriptive of the peculiar demand of the revolution, — an express affirmation of the right of secession. If we may infer anything from their reticence on this point, it is that they were not willing to expose their own Confederacy to the blows of the same weapon which they found had such facile power to destroy that they were casting off. They, at least, were willing to leave an expressed right of secession open to future advisement, and allow the question, in the mean time, to float upon the varying tide of construction. I venture to prophesy that as their experience grows older, and their sovereign *harmonies* are more and more tested, they will be less and less inclined to honor the doctrine with a clause in their constitution. Certainly we may infer from this omission that the failure of *our* Constitution to recognize this right does not present the gravamen for which they have plunged the country into rebellion. I would not charge that numerous body of gentlemen — whom I have referred to in a former letter as the long and persistent denouncers of secession as treason — with a vagary so extravagant as that. As the matter stands now, it is evident that the rebel Convention at Montgomery were not fully prepared to vindicate their zeal in their professed faith, by testifying to it in their works when the opportunity for the first time was presented to them.

Notwithstanding these few alterations, the Government rejected and the Government adopted are so entirely the same in all their leading features and minor details, and especially so identical in their capacities for good or evil administration, that it is very clear this revolution was not inaugurated to get rid of any existing grievance or tyrannical authority resulting from the Constitution of the United States.

We are left, then, to seek in the *administration* of the Government, the source of the differences which, it is supposed, could only be satisfactorily adjusted by a dissolution of the Union.

Upon this point I might remark, in passing, that it would take a very strong case of wrongs inflicted by the administration of a Government — whose administration is changeable at brief periods by the act of the people themselves, and always under the control of popular representation in which the whole nation has a voice, — it would be necessary to make a very strong case of continued and persevering oppression, through such an administration, to justify a resort to the terrible process of relief found in civil war.

When we ask the question, "Has the South been impelled to adopt this extreme remedy of revolution, by the galling tyranny practised upon it through years of unmitigated suffering by the oppressive temper of the majority, exhibited in a constant course of hostile administration?" we have an answer in the fact, that from the 4th of March, 1789, until the 4th of March, 1861, the administration of public affairs has been almost wholly in Southern hands.

We have had, during that period, fifteen Presidents, of which nine were native Southern men, three natives of New England, two of New York, and one of Pennsylvania; of those which were not natives of the Slave States three were Democrats, of whom the South was wont to boast as " Northern men with Southern principles," and were distinctly chosen and elected by Southern influence; of the remaining three two were Whigs, distinguished for their equitable administration and irreproachable performance of their duty, in which they received the efficient support of the whole Whig party of the South. The only President, in all that space of seventy-two years, who might be plausibly charged with a Northern bias in his administration was the elder Adams, the companion of Washington, and the incumbent of the presidential office for but one term, at the close of the last century. It may be also remarked, that from the 4th of March, 1801, when it may be said that parties became distinctively organized, down to the 4th of March, 1861, a period of sixty years, the Government was administered by Southern Presidents for forty-one years, and by Presidents born in the Free States nineteen years.

During the whole of this latter period of sixty years the representation in both Houses of Congress is to be noted for a preponderance of Southern influence in the control of the policy of Government, maintained, in part, through the numerical strength of the Southern vote, and, still more decisively, by the party predilections of the Democratic members.

It is vain, therefore, in the view of these facts, to suppose that this rebellion can pretend to any justifiable cause arising out of the ordinary, legitimate, and habitual administration of the Government.

Where, then, shall we seek for that beadroll of wrongs which the enlightened justice of mankind in this age demands from every people who meditate a recourse to arms against established authority? What is the provocation which may be rightfully pleaded in the great forum of national judgment, still more, before the awful tribunal of Heaven, for this dreadful assault upon the social order, yea, upon the very existence of the grandest and most prosperous of Commonwealths?

Even to this day we have seen no clear and intelligible proclamation of the real motives which impelled this outbreak. Speculation, both here and in Europe, gropes blindly through a maze of conjectures to make a plausible theory for this extraordinary phenomenon. Prizes are offered for essays to explain it. The gravest and the lightest reasons are assigned to it. It is the terrible plague spot of slavery; it is the trivial discomfort of incompatible temper; it is commercial tariffs; navigation laws; unequal distribution of patronage; disappointed ambition; provincial antipathies; "*quot homines tot sententiæ.*" Why is there not some solemn and earnest State paper put forth, in "decent respect for the opinions of mankind," which shall solve these doubts? We have had more than one ostentatious attempt of this kind, but they all fail to rise to the dignity of an excuse. They do not agree with each other. They present no consistent specific statement of injuries inflicted upon the South by the Government, to which the whole people in revolt can refer as their defence for taking up arms, or which sensible men might not be ashamed to avow as a justifiable motive for revolution.

We find it hard to reconcile the inauguration of a rebellion of such magnitude as this, with our own estimate of the insufficiency of the excuse for it, and our previous knowledge of the respectability, both in character and intelligence, of many of the individuals concerned in getting it up. We make every allowance for pride and prejudice, for ambition, for excitability of temper, for extravagance of political theory, and all the other influences which may disturb an honest judgment, but there still remains the problem, — Why did men of ordinary ability and forethought, to say nothing of men of larger scope, enter upon an adventure of such fearful import as this? The question has often been asked, Have they presented any grievance which a dissolution of the Union would remove; in fact, not make worse? The inadequacy of the reasons given for the instalment of this momentous struggle would compel us to believe, if we did not, from our own observation of events, know it before, that the ostensible causes are not the real ones, and that we must seek elsewhere for the true exposition of the movement.

We feel no surprise at the rapid spread of the rebellion through the South, after it was once set on foot. However much we may lament the width and tenacity of its grasp, and the fatal aberration into which it has drawn many estimable persons, amongst whom we recognize friends we shall ever think of with regret, we cannot but regard their defection as the natural sequence of the great primal wrong which brought them into such a temptation, and we shall never abandon the hope that the same facility of yielding which carried them astray, will be equally apt, when the occasion may serve, to bring them back. I have hinted, in a former letter, at the category in which they are placed. I know that it is the nature of all rebellion to be constantly making a new case for its reinforcement; and it scarcely fails to happen, that the multitudes who are swept into its train are unable to resist the motives they find for complicity presented to them in the disorders which the violence of war, the emergencies of State, and the inevitable invasions of personal comfort and private right bring upon themselves or the communities in which they live. As passion rises reason subsides, and the minds of excitable men become all aglow with the indignation of present griefs. It is enough for them that injuries — which a calm reflection would show them to be the necessary and natural concomitants of civil commotion, and for which, therefore, the authors of the commotion themselves are responsible — are perpetrated within their view; it is enough for them that the Government, whilst reeling under the blows of the rebellion, resorts to its highest prerogative of defence, and wields an unaccustomed power against the treason that strikes at its life; they are filled with resentment at the present calamity, and at the use of force to conquer revolt, and do not pause to consider the awful crime which hurls these disasters upon society, nor the sacred duty which rebellion casts upon the Government to preserve itself from destruction. Man grows selfish when terrors surround him, and the first instinct, even of the brave, is to fly to the protection of their friends before they will lift an arm for their country. This is natural to the common herd of mankind. It is only from the truly heroic, from those who possess that rare wisdom which discerns the path of duty with vision undisturbed by passion or affection, and who have the courage to follow it, we may expect an example of that noblest patriotism which accounts our country dearer than all other human blessings, and its service only subordinate to that we owe our Creator. We are not surprised, therefore, that the thoughtless, the ignorant, or the impulsive members of an excited community lose sight of the grandeur of a national cause and become the assertors and champions of the meaner but more intelligible quarrel of the neighborhood, the district, or the section. Unhappily it is so ordained that the fate of empire does not rest in the hands of the wise, the good, and the valiant, without a counterpoise, more or less hurtful, from the foolish, the vicious, and the weak.

It is not from this crowd of followers in the track of revolution that we may hope to procure an intelligible exposition of its origin or its aims. They can only give us their own personal aggravations, or, at best, the delusions which have kindled their enthusiasm and bewildered their reason. But from those who first conceived the design and gave it headway, and who still assume to shape and direct its progress, we have to exact a more rigorous responsibility, and hold them accountable to public judgment, if they can offer no adequate and upright justification for the desolation they have cast into the bosom of the country, and for the terrible issues of the conflict. They have not yet done so. That their enterprise admits of no such defence I shall endeavor to show in the further prosecution of this inquiry.

LETTER VI.

REVOLUTION.

OCTOBER, 1863.

THE aspiration of Southern ambition, which has reached to the climax of rebellion, was not the growth of a month or a year. Those who have watched the course of public events, and noted the development of opinion in the South for years past, have seen many signs of the coming peril; and, if the country was not prepared for it, it was not for want of an occasional warning. Everybody knew there were restless spirits in the South who would rejoice in the opportunity to destroy the Union, and that these were endeavoring to create a sectional sentiment that might favor the accomplishment of their wish. But the common faith of the country in the patriotism of the people of the South, and the profound conviction of the whole North, and we may say also of the larger part of the Southern communities, that no motive existed which could possibly stir up the people of any State to the mad enterprise of assailing the integrity of the Union, dispelled every apprehension on this score. The public generally regarded the danger as a chimera. Even the Government, which ought to have been distrustful enough to put itself on guard, seemed to be utterly unconscious of the gathering trouble. Never was a country taken so much at unawares.

The year 1860 was one of great prosperity. The nation exhibited something more than its customary light-heartedness, and had risen into a tone of hilarity from the peculiar excitements of the year. The spring was occupied with celebrations of the advent of the Japanese Embassy, which signalized the enlargement of our commerce with the East, and autumn was filled with pageants to welcome the heir of the British throne, whose visit was regarded as an event of national congratulation that promised long peace and happy fellowship with the world, — a token of new strength and greater influence to the Republic. It was a year distinguished by public demonstrations of faith and hope in the future destiny of the country. Few persons were willing to believe, or allowed themselves to think, that, whilst we were thus increasing the popularity of the nation abroad, and inaugurating an era of remarkable promise to the advantage of our foreign and domestic interests, there was any considerable party amongst us who could harbor the parricidal design of crushing these brilliant hopes in the destruction of the country itself, or that the band of political agitators, to whom the public was accustomed to impute such a design, could so infatuate their followers as to prevail with them to attempt it. It was in this state of confident security, and in the very midst of these peaceful manifestations, that the storm broke upon the country.

Notwithstanding this dissonance between the tone of public feeling at that time, and the terrific incident which grated upon it with such inopportune discord, the rebellion came as a predestined feat. The year, the month, almost the week of its explosion, had been determined in councils held long before, and the plot broke into action at its appointed time, to surprise and discomfit, with a sudden shock, the peaceful temper of the Government and its friends.

It was preordained that the Presidential Election of 1860 should supply the *occasion* and the *day*, though it did not supply the motive for this wicked attempt against the life of the nation.

Let us endeavor to extract from the history of the times, and from our own knowledge of the course of events, what we can find to explain the inducements that moved the actors in this terrible tragedy.

It has grown to be an almost universally accepted fact, on the northern side of Mason and Dixon's line, that this rebellion owes its origin simply to a sense of danger to the institution of slavery aroused in the Southern mind by the political agitations of the question of its value, which have engrossed so much of the public attention during the last thirty years; and that, to avert this danger, the South had resolved upon separation from the North.

I think this view of the origin of our troubles much too narrow. Slavery, of itself and for itself, is not the cause of the rebellion. I do not believe that there was one intelligent, leading, and thinking man in the South, when this rebellion broke out, who imagined that slavery was in any kind of danger either from the action of the National Government or the State Governments; nor that it could be successfully assailed by the hostility that was exhibited against it in the public or private opinion of Northern society. I think that Southern statesmen were and are perfectly convinced that the Government of the United States, embracing both National and State organizations, afforded an impregnable security to the institution of slavery which no power on this continent, in its lawful course of administration, could disturb: and, moreover, that the guarantees which these organizations combined offer to that institution are not only entirely adequate to its protection, but are such as no government ever before supplied, and such, also, as no government, of the same scope of jurisdiction and power, would ever again agree to make. It is the merest sham and make-believe for any Southern man to pretend that the institution of slavery was ever brought into peril before this rebellion exposed it to the dangers that now surround it. I can hardly suppose that any man of sense in the South could believe otherwise than that a war, once provoked between the States, would be the only effective agency which could destroy or impair it against the will and without the coöperation of the Slave States themselves.

That the slave interest has been domineering and aggressive in its endeavor to control the administration of the public affairs of the Union, is a fact of common observation; and that it has been exceedingly reluctant to part with this power of control, as the gradually increasing strength of its antagonist element in the nation made it apparent that it must soon do, is equally true. If we add to these considerations the influence of slavery upon the character, habits, and social life of the ruling class of Southern citizens, we may perceive the degree and extent in which it may be regarded as the *causa causans* of the rebellion, in the minds of certain ambitious men who assumed to direct Southern opinion, and who, acting in concert, plotted and executed this great act of treason.

It is, at the same time, true that slavery may be reckoned as the *immediate* cause of the war, in the estimate of a very considerable portion of the Southern people. Danger to the security of slave property furnished a taking watchword to a large and influential class of these. The phantom of negro equality, which haunts the imagination of the lower stratum of Southern society, furnished another not less potent for mischief. These topics were adroitly handled to excite the passions and alarm the fears of both the upper and under sections of these impressible communities, and were found very effective in mustering men into the ranks of revolt. They were discussed as popular motives to rebellion, and used to give it a plausible justification. They supplied a ready argument adapted to the prejudice or mental capacity of the several parties to whom it was addressed, and they especially served to familiarize the people with the thought of breaking up the Union.

These agitations of the slave question had something of the same effect upon portions of the people of the North; for the aversion to the Union was not alone harbored in the South. I have no doubt that the extreme opinions on this subject, preached and written by a sect in New England, had a most pernicious influence in extending the thought of dissolution through the South. There was an equal fanaticism on both sides, quite as evident in favor of slavery in one section as against it in the other. Secessionists and abolitionists, in the ultra phases of their respective demands, were in full accord as to the ultimate remedy of the grievances they imagined themselves to suffer. It was curious to see how, in ascending the gamut of their opposite extravagances, the two parties kept pace with each other on the scale, of which the highest note on each side was disunion. Both North and South were, at the beginning, in harmony in admitting slavery to be a social evil which was to be considerately dealt with and abandoned when that could be done without injury to existing interests. From this point Southern enthusiasts diverged in one direction, Northern in another. With one, slavery rose to be asserted successively as a harmless utility, as a blessing, a divine institution, and, finally, as " the corner-stone rejected by the builders," upon which a new dynasty was to be constructed, and our old cherished Union to be dashed into fragments. With the other, slavery, passing through equal grades, was declared to be a disgrace; a great national sin; a special curse of Heaven; and, at last, a stigma that made the Union "a covenant of hell," and which, therefore, should be shattered to atoms to give place to another order of polity. The two opposite lines thus converged in the same point, — that of dissolution. This is the extreme boundary to which a passionate monomania conducted the agitations of thirty years of the subject of slavery. The irritation produced by this persevering and angry reverberation of the question, from side to side, undoubtedly prepared the people of the South for the explosion of 1860, and equally prepared the people of the North for a prompt resentment against it, and thus misled the popular opinion on both sides to regard the slavery question as the immediate source of the attempt at revolution. But the contrivers, the heads and leaders of the scheme, had a much deeper purpose than the removal of any imagined danger to the security of the institution. They took advantage of the common sensibility of their people on this subject to aid them in a design of much wider import.

It is only necessary to note the solicitude with which Southern politicians of the last and present generation have contemplated the invasion of their supremacy in the Government, and the importunate zeal with which they have insisted upon preserving an equilibrium between Free and Slave States, — meaning by that the *preponderance* of Southern influence, — to be convinced that the perpetuity of their control of the Administration has been the leading idea of their policy. The threat of disunion has been the customary persuasion by which they have, from time to time, endeavored to subdue the first symptoms of disaffection to their ascendency. This had become the familiar terror of every Presidential canvass since the great flurry of Nullification in 1832, and, in fact, its frequency had made it so stale, that when, at last, the danger was really imminent, the country was incredulous of the event, as much from derision of the threat as a worn-out trick, as from the common conviction that no cause had arisen to provoke it.

Looking at the various pretexts upon which, as occasion prompted, this disunion was threatened, — the tariff, the navigation laws, the distribution of patronage, the Texas question, the admission of California, the Kansas organization, the Territories, — all of which have been used in turn by the Cotton States to frighten the nation with the danger of rupture, we have in these the most perspicuous guide to the true motives of the breach of 1861. The fact was then at last demonstrated, that the hour was at hand when other interests in the country were to have a hearing and an influence, and that the majority of the nation meant to govern it;

that the South must take its due and proper place in the Union and relinquish its ambition of undivided empire. That long-feared and long warded-off day had come, and with it came the first real, unfeigned, absolute purpose of the partisan politicians of the Southern States in combination, to separate the South from the North, and to attempt to build up a power at home, in which Southern politics and Southern ambition should have undisputed sway. The Union was enjoyed as long as it ministered to the ascendency of the Planting States, but was to be cast off as soon as the nation reached that epoch in its progress at which it was able to release itself from the thraldom of sectional control, and to regulate its policy in accordance with the demands of the general welfare.

Never was that selfishness which is the characteristic sin of sectional politicians, more offensively demonstrated than in the alacrity with which the prominent men of these Planting States — I mean especially to designate, by this term, that region which is devoted to the production of cotton, rice, and sugar — combined to destroy the unity, and, as they hoped, the strength, and even the very existence, of this nation, at the first moment when the opportunity promised them a chance of success. Their cool repudiation, not only of the obligations of honorable citizenship, but also of the simple gratitude due to a commonwealth of brethren of the same family, which had watched over them in their days of weakness, and nursed them into the full vigor of manhood, and which had, moreover, conferred upon them all the political importance they had ever attained, — this act will stand forever prominent in the history of this sad time, as the darkest blot the rebellion will leave upon the character of its most conspicuous contrivers and agents. Think of the trivial pretences and the positive treachery of those States purchased, created, and reared by the Union, — Florida, Louisiana, Texas, Arkansas! Think of the good example, the good faith, and the nice sense of honor of those older States which persuaded these to strike at the heart of the beneficent parent who had given them existence, protection, and a heritage of matchless prosperity! Think of the obligations which these States owe to the Union, and then inquire into the real motives which tempted them to bring down upon the nation the terrible calamity of civil war!

We shall look in vain, as I have before remarked, for this motive in any right denied the States by the National Government, or any privilege withheld which State or individual citizen might lawfully or reasonably demand.

But, supposing there were some wrong inflicted by the Government, in the course of its administration, upon one or more of the States, and — to put the case of opposition upon its strongest ground — supposing the right of secession to be acknowledged as the lawful resort of a State, certainly we may say, in view of the special compact of the Constitution, and of the plighted faith of the people of every State to stand to and abide by all the responsibilities and duties created by the common National Government, every consideration of justice, as well as of propriety and self-respect, would impose upon the complaining party the necessity of making a deliberate and friendly appeal to the rest of the nation for redress through the means provided by law. How much more imperative is the obligation of such appeal when no right of secession is contained in the compact, and when the proceeding, unless sanctioned by the general consent of the nation, could only be classed in the category of revolution? To make a decent case of justification for revolution, every tribunal of moral law or enlightened opinion would hold that, as a preliminary fact, that consent should be asked and refused; and, moreover, that the insurgent party should be able to show such a violation of compact by the offending government, as to produce intolerable oppression for which no remedy was to be found but that of separation.

Now, nothing is more clear than that neither of these conditions existed. There was no consent sought for or expected, but, on the contrary, a haste in rushing into rebellion, which one might almost believe was intended to prevent the risk of either consent or conciliation.

There was no intolerable oppression, or, indeed, oppression of any kind. The utmost point to which any mover of the sedition went, was to affirm that it was feared there might be some oppression hereafter, — though that was not very intelligibly made out in the result of the Presidential election, which proved the successful party to be in a minority of the whole vote of the country. We had heard, it is true, a great deal about the iniquity of import duties and protection of domestic industry, but these were only the common resources of all

Governments, and, indeed, when it concerned Southern interests, were the special requisitions of Southern policy; as, for example, in the invariable demand from the South for the protection of sugar and cotton, — to say nothing of the protection insisted upon by the South for our early cotton manufacture.

We had heard a complaint that the bounty of the Government had fallen in stinted measure upon the South in the expenditures of the revenue; but the fact was that the public treasure was applied in that section to the establishment of forts, arsenals, navy-yards, hospitals, custom-houses, mints, and other public structures, quite as liberally as they were needed, and certainly without any idea of unjust discrimination; whilst, in addition to these expenditures, enormous amounts, far greater than were appropriated to any other section, were expended in the purchase and defence of Southern territory.

We had heard a great deal said about the injustice of Congress in refusing to allow the extension of slavery into the territories north of the Compromise line; indeed, this was magnified, at last, into the chief provocation to the war. But quite apart from the political folly and the moral atrocity of planting slavery afresh, and with premeditated design, in free communities, it is to be remarked as a very notable fact, in connection with this as a ground of quarrel, that the Missouri Compromise was, itself, a Southern measure, and its passage hailed throughout the South as a signal victory. It is also worthy of note, that, from the beginning of the Government, Southern statesmen have refused to allow slavery to go north of that line, 36° 30′, in the Territories; and that the Northwestern Territory, embracing all the Western States north of the line, was made inviolably free soil by the demand of Virginia, through Mr. Jefferson, and by the support of Southern votes.

We may pursue this inquiry through all the history of the past, and we shall find that all these topics of complaint against the Government, which have furnished themes for popular discourse and irritation of the Southern mind, and which, for more than a quarter of a century, have been urged as incentives to disunion, are but pretexts employed as lures to entrap the ignorant, or as devices to stimulate the sedition of men who welcome anything that may give plausibility to a foregone purpose of revolt.

The pursuit of independence by these confederated States has a very different aim from the redress of such shallow griefs as these.

Whoever shall be able hereafter to reveal the secret history of those various conclaves which have held counsel on the repeated attempts to invade and conquer, — or, as the phrase was, liberate Cuba; whoever shall unfold the schemes of seizing Nicaragua, of aiding revolution in Mexico, of possessing Sonora, will make some pretty sure advances in disclosing the true pathway to the sources of this rebellion. The organization of the Knights of the Golden Circle, and their spread over the country; their meetings and transactions; who managed them and set them on to do their appointed work, — whoever shall penetrate into the midnight which veiled this order from view, will also open an authentic chapter in the history of this outbreak.

There was a great scheme of dominion in this plot. The fancy of certain Southern politicians was dazed with a vision of Empire. Years have been rolling on whilst this brilliant scheme was maturing in their private councils, and at intervals startling the nation by some unexpected eruption. The design, which lay too deep in darkness to be penetrated by the uninitiated, occasionally rose to the surface in some bold and rash adventure, which either the vigilance of Government, or the imperfect means of success which the necessity of concealment imposed upon it, rendered abortive. The Cuban expeditions miscarried; the Sonora failed; the Nicaragua forays were defeated,— all these chiefly by the careful watch of the Government. Large sums of money were squandered in these fruitless adventures, and many lives were lost. Worse than these mishaps, eager hopes were disappointed and long-indulged dreams dissipated. It was found that the Union was in the way; that the National Government was the impediment; and that, as long as the South was bound to obey that Government, these cherished schemes would be always certain to miscarry. This experience turned the hostility of thwarted ambition against the Union, and directed the thoughts of these agents of mischief towards its destruction.

Then came the next movement. There is, I think, a better foundation than mere rumor for saying that overtures were made, before the rebellion broke out, to the Emperor of the French for support and patronage in the scheme; that a very alluring picture was presented to him of a great Southern Confederacy, to embrace the land of cotton, of sugar, of coffee, of the most precious tobaccoes, and of the choicest fruits, of the most valuable timber, and the richest mines, — comprehending the Gulf States, Cuba, St. Domingo, and other islands, Mexico, Central America, and perhaps reaching even beyond into the borders of South America, — a great tropical and semi-tropical paradise of unbounded affluence of product, secured by an impregnable monopoly created by Nature. This large domain was to be organized into one Confederate Government, and provided with the cheapest and most docile and submissive of all labor; its lands were to be parcelled into principalities, and landlords were to revel in the riches of Aladdin's lamp. This was the grand idea which the Emperor was solicited to patronize with his protection, for which he was to be repaid in treaty arrangements, by which France should enjoy a free trade in the products of French industry, and precedence in gathering the first fruits of all this wealth of culture. Certainly a very dazzling lure this, to the good will of the Emperor!

It is said the Emperor was quite captivated with the first view of this brilliant project, but on riper deliberation was brought to a pause. The scheme, he discovered, stood on one leg: the whole structure rested on slavery, which was much too ricketty a support to win favor in this nineteenth century with the shrewdest of European statesmen. The plot was "too light for the counterpoise of so great an opposition." The structure might last a few years, but very soon it would tumble down and come to nought. And so, it is whispered, the Emperor declined the venture. This is a bit of secret history which time may or may not verify. From some inklings of that day which escaped into open air, I believe it true. We heard various boastings, in the summer of 1860, of French support to the threatened separation, and there were agents in Europe negotiating for it. During all that preliminary period there was a great deal said in the South about reviving the slave-trade. When the Emperor refused, this was suddenly dropped and England was then looked to as the ally in the coming revolt. Abolition England was to be won by another strategy. The Montgomery Convention asserted a clause in the Confederate Constitution forbidding the slave-trade, and, oddly enough for a government founded on the central idea of slavery, the commissioners who represented it in England were authorized to assure the British Minister that it was really the old Government which was fighting to perpetuate slavery, whilst the new one was only seeking free trade; thereby gently insinuating a disinterested indifference on the slave question, which might ultimately come into full accord with England on that subject. These revelations stand in strange contrast with the popular theme that has rushed so many into the rebellion. As the matter now rests, the rebel Government has quite platform enough to be as pro-slavery or as anti-slavery as its European negotiations may require; and if these should utterly fail, there is nothing in the constitutional provision to interrupt the African slave-trade a single day. For what is that provision worth in a region where neither courts nor juries would execute the law?

Whilst this grand idea of tropical extension was seething in the brain of the leaders, and their hopes of fruition were vivid, the plan was to confine the revolt to the Cotton States,— or, at least, to give the Border States a very inferior rôle in the programme. They might come in when all was adjusted, but were to have no share in the primary organization. Every one remembers how these Border States were flouted in the beginning, and told they were not fit to be consulted, and that the only advantage they could bring to the Southern Confederacy was that of serving as a frontier to prevent the escape of slaves. But when the original plan was found to be a failure, the views of the managers were changed; the Border States became indispensable to any hope of success, and the most active agencies of persuasion, force, and fraud were set in motion to bring them in. How mournfully did it strike upon the heart of the nation when Virginia, in the lead of this career of submission, sank to the humiliation of pocketing the affront that had been put upon her, and consented to accept a position which nothing but the weakness of her new comrades induced them to allow her!

Since the hope of this broader dominion has come to an end, the rebellion is still persistently pursued for the accomplishment of its secondary objects. There is still, doubtless, some residuary expectation that, even without foreign patronage, in the event of success, this desire of extension of territory may in time be gratified; but it is no longer the chief object of pursuit. The pride of the South, its resentment, its rage, are all now enlisted in pushing forward to whatever consummation they may imagine to be attainable. They now insist on independence from the very hatred their disappointments have engendered. But they seek it, too, as the only method left for the maintenance of that class domination which they have ever enjoyed, and which they are now unwilling to surrender.

LETTER VII.

REBELLION.

JANUARY, 1864.

IN the preceding letters I have had occasion to say much of Secession and Revolution, and to show the different categories in which they respectively place the war waged by the South. It requires no great insight to perceive the relation which these two ideas, considered as motives of conduct, have to the question of mere right and wrong in this conflict. In that view they have a notable significance, and stand very wide apart. I recur to them now to make some remarks on that point, and to note the alternate use the partisans of the South have made of these two topics as persuasives in aid of their project to destroy the Union.

By the opportune use of both, as occasion favored, they have increased the popularity of their cause. They would have failed if they had been compelled to present it to their people singly, upon either of the two. Neither secession alone, nor revolution alone, would have found that undivided support which is essential to success. In that storm of excitement raised by their chiefs at the beginning of the strife, and in the flurry of that vainglorious, and, I might say, insolent spirit of defiance, — that contemptuous disparagement of the North as a selfish, vulgar, and craven people, over whom they promised an easy victory and a short war, — the Southern masses were hurried along into the irrevocable step of rebellion. Few stopped to weigh the excuse for such a step, but listened with willing ear to every pretext, however false or feeble, in its justification, which partisanship or political bigotry could suggest. The multitude were incapable of any accurate or conscientious opinion on the subject; all were anxious to take a quick part in the coming fray, not doubting for a moment that the preordained feat was to be accomplished with little more expenditure of means than the show of force and a swaggering boast of certain triumph. Thus it came that we saw the instant exhibition of that martial array, which astonished the world by its magnitude and the sober thinking people of the Loyal States by its madness. All that host which came into the field, and that great reserve which stood behind it at home, claimed the vindication of their conduct on one or the other of these motives, — often in the avowal of both. They professed secession, or revolution, or both, quite indifferent to the moral responsibility inferred by either.

I have observed many persons, whose previous education and habit of opinion had committed them against the doctrine of secession, seizing with avidity upon what they were glad to call *a right* of revolution, too plainly as a mere salvo to bring their easily satisfied consciences into accord with their foregone resolve to embark in the rebellion. They imagined they had found a complete justification in so wretched a self-deceit as this, even for a deed so portentous as that of rending their country into fragments. They did not deign to ask themselves the question whether their revolution had a single plea to redeem it from the disgrace of an immeasurable crime. It was enough to call it "revolution," and thenceforth treason became transmuted into a virtue. "You are very much mistaken, sir," said a young Marylander, conversing with an acquaintance in Washington, just after the famous nineteenth of April, speaking with exultation of that bloody scene in the streets of Baltimore, in which citizen soldiers, whilst peaceably marching through, in obedience to law and in the performance of honorable duty, were ferociously set upon and murdered, — the young spokesman himself scarcely concealing his own participation in the affair, but describing it as a heroic exploit, — " You are much mistaken when you call this a riot. No, sir; it is a *revolution!* Maryland does not go for secession, she goes for revolution." All thought of crime had, of course, vanished from his mind. His heart was full of war. He was ready to desolate every field in Maryland and convert her chief city into a blackened ruin. Revolution — with what excuse for it! — had been installed. The next step was to make it glorious with carnage.

With such a flippant and silly casuistry as this, how many thousands have imbrued their hands in the blood of their brethren!

I have seen others, not quite bold enough to outface the opinion of the community in which they lived, by an open avowal of a purpose of revolution — there being still some prudent suspicion that the people of the neighborhood were not yet maddened up to the delusion of believing in the *tyranny* of our free Government — who have gradually slid into the doctrine of secession, as the only shift left them to gratify a love for political excitement, and to furnish a pretext for joining the ranks of comrades who had fired their imagination with visions of honor and hopes of personal reward to be won over the prostrate body of their country. In such case the feeble plea of secession — once called the *peaceful* process of change — was held to justify all the wild violence which preluded and challenged the measures taken by the Government for its own defence.

I will not say that there are not large numbers of persons in the South who have given their aid to this destructive war on more honest grounds. It is not credible that, in a conflict of such momentous issues, whole communities should rush into it with such earnest zeal as stirs the heart of the Southern States, and should pursue it with such brave perseverance, through such an experience of suffering and sacrifice as we now witness, without being sustained by some very vivid conviction of right and duty. We know too well, and deplore too poignantly, the fact that in those ranks are found many men adorned with the best qualities that inspire respect and confidence. Their armies and their councils are full of them. They do us a great injustice if they think we underrate either their sincerity or their personal worth. How joyously would we welcome them back to that brotherhood which they have so recklessly broken! But all history warns us that the virtue of strife is not to be judged by the fervor of its champions nor by the earnestness of their convictions. A false principle, unhappily, more potently invokes the intemperate vindication of mankind than a true one. It wages a fiercer war; although, in the end, it is surest of overthrow. When it is brought into conflict with the sentiment of a society as powerful as its own, the very hazard of its assertion presents a danger which exaggerates it into a passion that so distempers the mind as to make reflection hopeless. Many good men of the South have been swept from their feet by this impulse as by a whirlwind.

It is very difficult to find the means of friendly approach, in a rebellion like this, to the class of men I have just described, — men who, with honest convictions, have fallen into the error of false opinion, through temperament or local influence or some ply of early education. The wrong-headed are proverbially obstinate, even in the debates of tranquil life; they are proportionately hopeless of persuasion in the great turmoils of public affairs, when passion stimulates the heart and inflames the pride of the mind.

In looking to this description of really earnest champions of the South, we shall find them, like the others, divided between the two motives to which I have referred.

There are not a few of the most authoritative of these champions who, by some strange aberration which almost amounts to an idiosyncrasy, have grown up in the conscientious belief that our national Union was never, and never meant to be, anything better than a rope of sand, — the feeblest voluntary compact, unguarded by a single defence against the superior power of the States; that no one owed it allegiance, — not even the poor respect of reverence; that no *State* owed it obedience any further than suited its own convenience. Such a fancy must naturally engender contempt for the Union whenever a contingency should arise to bring it into conflict with State pretension.

We may trace this extraordinary doctrine to

a political vice which has been nursed in the peculiar constitution of Southern society, and which has given the predominant hue to all characteristic Southern opinion; that most pernicious vice of an exorbitant and engrossing State pride, — a sentiment, which we may say, is not only dangerous, but fatal to any just estimate or conception of the national supremacy.

I do not stop here to consider the source, the extent or the influences of this sentiment. I have only to remark, that it takes hold of much of the Southern mind with the grasp and quality of a great egotism, creating an emotion of self-glorification in those who foster it, and breeding ideas of sectional and personal superiority which make them jealous of the National Government, and, in a certain sense, unfriendly to all who look upon that Government as a paramount power. They habitually degrade the Union in the common esteem of their circle, reduce their politics to the standard of a narrow provincialism, and disqualify themselves for that comprehensive statesmanship which embraces catholic love of country.

We have been accustomed in past time — long before this sad commotion had ruffled the surface of our peaceful life — to smile at some of the phases of character which this sentiment had impressed upon a class of country gentlemen very frequently encountered in the older States of the South. Many a man of this worshipful order, jocund and complacent in the patriarchal dignity conferred by hereditary bondsmen and acres, has been pleasantly noted, in those innocent days, for a constitutional dogmatism on the question of the sovereignty of the State, and for the radiant self-satisfaction with which he was wont to demonstrate the shallowness of that pestilent fallacy which, he affirmed, so often misled the logic of Congress and muddled the brains of Webster and Clay, — and even, he was sorry to believe, of Marshall and Madison, — the fallacy, namely, of supposing that the United States could lawfully aspire to the grandeur of a nation. Centralization was the phantom which appeared especially to haunt the minds of these worthy gentlemen. "We are plunging into the gulf of centralization," was their common warning. If, in making this dogma clear, they were somewhat incomprehensible or even tedious, they were always earnest and, in their own judgment, infallible.

But whilst this State pride did no greater harm, in our earlier and happier era, than the producing this crop of impracticable dialecticians, whose obstructive philosophy was constantly overleaped by the general good sense of the nation, and whom the country could afford to endure, and even to flatter, for the good-natured vanity of their opinions, it has, in this later and sadder day, converted its once innocuous votaries into seditious plotters against the common peace, and, by rapid transition, into fierce soldiers and implacable rebels. It has now become apparent that this excessive pride of State has been silently, for half a century or more, sowing the seeds of that dreadful strife of which the present generation is reaping the harvest.

All of this class of thinkers — whom I have sought to characterize by their extravagant devotion to a distorted ideal of the ascendant position of the State in our political system, and by their personal sentiment of State pride and its corollaries of State rights, as these are magnified by the lens of Southern opinion — are, by natural consequence and fair deduction from their antecedents, out-and-out Secessionists, honestly consistent in their faith, and do not pretend to, or desire, other justification for their participation in the present disturbance, than that which they find in their own philosophy.

There is another class, the counterpart to these, equally sincere in their conviction, wholly opposed to this theory of secession, wholly unstricken by this inordinate estimate of the State, who are afflicted with a hallucination even more mischievous. They are men who have wrought themselves to the belief that the National Government has already grown to be a monster of such horrid proportions and propensities as to be no longer endurable by a free people; that it has been perverted — to use their own language — into " a consolidated despotism," under the pressure of whose malignant power all liberty, civil and religious, is doomed to be crushed out; that the representative system no longer affords space for the expression of the popular will as a defence against executive ambition; that State organizations are no longer barriers against national encroachments, and that the President and his party are not only the absolute lords of the ascendant, but that their power is destined to be perpetual and universal. Such are the spectres that have affrighted the imagination of these men and moved them to the melancholy conviction that nothing short of a bloody revolution can rescue them and their generations from the grasp of this inexorable tyranny. Nothing, therefore, in their view, is more righteous, manly, and patriotic than a stern appeal to the sword as a redress for their wrongs. In this excited temper they rush into the *melée* of revolution, with the sincere hope of being able to regain their lost liberties in a New Confederacy enlightened and sustained by the tolerant and freedom-loving nature of Southern opinion, — and founded on the sacred corner-stone of unlimited African slavery!

Both of these opposite groups of thinkers are now profoundly in earnest in this conflict, and, what is certainly calculated to excite the wonder of an unconcerned spectator, are quite in harmony with each other, acting together for a common end, apparently unconscious of their divergence of creed, and the trouble they might expect to find, in the event of success, to administer to their mutual satisfaction the form of government they have unanimously adopted.

Now, it is to be remarked that, whilst the master spirits of this furious war have seen the value and taken advantage of these alternate agencies which have been so busy in stirring up the people to a revolt against the Government; and whilst they have lost no opportunity to encourage this variety of motive, and have plied every artifice of seduction or force to lure, drive, or drag impetuous manhood and credulous age, no less than pliant youth, into fatal alliance with the crime of treason, by every argument adapted to the prejudices, scruples, or different temperaments they had to deal with, they have themselves been cautious, in every public or official proclamation of their enterprise, to avoid any acknowledgment of a design of revolution. Whatever the intrinsic motive of their assault has been, however violent and revolutionary their proceeding, the official attitude they have assumed is that of States asserting their right to a peaceful and constitutional retirement from the National Union. They proclaim a right of secession as the sole basis of their action; whilst it is too unhappily evident that both their design and practice are revolution in its boldest and rudest form of exhibition. Their proclamation is intended for the world, and more especially for that European world whose sympathy they have evoked, whose aid they have expected, and whose moral support it was deemed all important to conciliate.

They were too astute not to perceive that — whilst their scheme was simply a design to destroy the Union by a daring and impious act of violence, and upon its ruins to construct a separate empire of their own, adapted to the polity suggested by their personal ambition and the greed of a fancied boundless wealth — they would hold a vantage ground in the great quarrel by keeping out of view every consideration which might infer their acknowledgment of a rebel position.

We may easily recount the obvious disadvantages which such an avowal would have thrown in their way, and which the secession theory — if the world could be persuaded to accredit it — would avoid.

First. The acknowledgment of a revolutionary movement would (as I have hitherto had occasion to remark) have carried the admission that they were the aggressors in the war; that war was contemplated by them as the necessary and premeditated means of their success, and was, consequently, an act of their own making, — for revolution always implies rebellion, and rebellion is war.

Second. It would have silenced at once that popular outcry against *coercion* which was found so effective, in the beginning of the quarrel, in exciting a prejudice against the Government, by charging it with the perpetration of a flagrant outrage against States that were merely asserting their constitutional rights. For rebellion being in its nature aggressive, every man would acknowledge that the Government would be but in the performance of its clearest duty in arraying the force of the country to resist the blow aimed at it and to punish the assailant. If there be any obligation more distinctly sanctioned by the concurrent opinion of mankind or the law of nations, and the neglect of which is stigmatized by a deeper disgrace than any other in the sphere of public duty, it is that which is demanded of every nation to protect the welfare of its people against "privy conspiracy, sedition, and rebellion," — those three grievous plagues of organized society against which the Church weekly invokes the deliverance of Heaven. If, therefore, the rebel leaders had announced their design as one of revolution, seeking to overthrow the laws and break up the established order of the Union by violent application of force, there was no man amongst them so obtuse as not to be capable of seeing how senseless must have been the complaint against the President for invoking the aid of the military power of the country to resist them.

Third. They knew that a scheme of revolution, being an appeal to those who are discontented with the Government to rebel against it, only addresses itself to such as believe in its expediency, and leaves all who do not assent to that expediency at liberty to refuse their aid; that this freedom of action would, in the first stages of the movement, have allowed a large portion of the people of the South the opportunity to stand firm to their loyalty, and refuse to take any share in the revolt against their country; whilst, on the secession theory, the State would act in its sovereign capacity, and, by declaring the separation complete, would *exact* the obedience of its citizens. In the first case, the citizen would regard himself as an individual free agent, with full liberty to decide upon his own conduct; in the latter, he would be overborne and coerced by a corporate authority claiming his allegiance and subordinating his individual will to what is called the public interest.

Fourth. Revolution also infers another and still more embarrassing right, — that of counter revolution. If the State may rebel against the National Government, why may not an aggrieved or discontented portion of the people of the State rebel against the State? Rebellion is a teacher of " bloody instructions " which may " return to plague the inventor." What argument can Virginia, for example, make in favor of a revolt against the authority of the Union, that may not be used with tenfold force by her own western counties to justify a revolt against her? Virginia herself had really no definable grievance against the Union. She was absolute mistress of her own domestic government, and could freely enact and execute all laws which she might deem necessary to her own welfare within her own limits. No human power could interfere with her there. She has never yet indicated a single item of grievance resulting from the acts of the Federal Government. In fact that Government has always been, in great part, in her own hands, or under the control of her influence. If she has not been happy and prosperous it is her own fault. I mean to say, she has no cause whatever to excuse her rebellion against the Union. Yet she revolted; we may say, gave to the revolution a countenance and support without which it would have speedily sunk into a futile enterprise. Having come into it, she assumed the right to compel her unwilling citizens to cast their lives and fortunes into the same issue. A large portion of her people, comprising the inhabitants of many counties in the mountain region of the Alleghanies, have always been distinguished — as, indeed, seems to be the characteristic of all our mountain country — for their strong attachment to the Union. These people have an aversion to slavery, and have been steadily intent upon establishing and expanding a system of free labor. They have, in fact, very little in common, either of sentiment or interest, with the governing power of the State. When, therefore, the question of secession was submitted to them, they voted against it. From that moment they were marked, and when the State, under the control of its lowland interest, raised the banner of revolt, its first movement was to invite the Southern army to occupy the mountain districts, to overawe and drive the people there, not only into submission to, the dominant power of the State, but into active hostility against the Union. To this end these loyal people were pursued with a bitter persecution, harried by a ruffian soldiery, hunted from their homes into the mountain fastnesses, their dwellings burnt, their crops destroyed, their fields laid waste, and every other cruelty inflicted upon them to which the savage spirit of revolution usually resorts to compel the consent of those who resist its command. The inhabitants of these beautiful mountain valleys are a simple, brave, and sturdy people, and all these terrors were found insufficient to force them into an act of treason. They refused, and in their turn revolted against this execrable tyranny and drew their swords in favor of the Union. What more natural or righteous than such a resistance? And yet, Virginia affects to consider this the deepest of crimes, and is continually threatening vengeance against what she calls these rebels: — Virginia, the rebel, denouncing rebellion!

Her own plea is, that she has only *seceded;* but Western Virginia *rebels.* There is a great difference!

The Southern Confederacy, like Virginia, sees this great difference in the two categories, and is quick enough to take advantage, as occasion serves, of that which suits its purpose.

The same state of things exists in Eastern Tennessee, in Western North Carolina, in Arkansas, and even in parts of Georgia and Alabama. Counter revolution would be rife in many districts, if the rebel Government did not suppress it with an iron hand, and subjugate the people by the presence of military force. Even this would be impossible if they had not insinuated into the popular mind of the South, as largely as they have done, the conviction of a right of secession, and persuaded the country that they were acting on that theory, and were but asserting the legitimate sovereignty of the States.

Western Virginia, for two years, endured the privation and suffering of this cruel and wicked attempt to enforce its submission and compel its people to abjure their earnest and eager allegiance to the Union — two years that left them without law, without any of the apparatus of government, helpless in everything but their own firm resolution and voluntary self-control as an orderly community; until, finding themselves under a necessity for organization, they erected their broken community into a government claiming its foundation in a just and righteous revolution, and in that character sought a place in the Union. Congress assented to their claim, and holding them, moreover, as loyal men, constituting a majority in number of the whole people of Virginia who retained a lawful citizenship in that State, accorded to them the right to express the voice of the State in favor of the division which thus gave a new member to the Union.

What lawful objection can the South make to this counter revolution, but the simple, and, in the actual state of the case, absurd idea that it is not itself pursuing a career of revolution, but only a constitutional right of secession?

Lastly, I may add to the considerations which have operated upon the mind of the Southern leaders in their endeavor to persuade the world that they are not amenable to the responsibilities of a rebellion, one which I have presented in a former letter, and which I briefly repeat here as necessary to the completeness of this summary. The inauguration of a rebellion imposes upon those who attempt it the necessity of showing a just cause for such an assault upon the peace of society. It must be no casual disturbance of the welfare of a district, no fancied possible wrong impending over the future, no motive of factious ambition, but a real, present, permanent element of actual or prospective discontent which is beyond the reach of peaceful redress through the appointed forms of amendment, but which is so radicated in the constitution of government that nothing short of forcible resistance can remove it. The writers in the interest of legitimacy, as that is understood in European law, say it must be a condition of intolerable and irremediable oppression. Our American doctrine does not go so far as that. We substitute for it a reasonable apprehension of an incurable perversion of government towards the invasion of public or private rights. And, even in that case, revolution cannot justly be resorted to until, by appeal to all the normal or appointed means of redress, it is proved that remedy is hopeless. Short of these conditions, revolution is the greatest of crimes, the blacker in proportion to the unreality of the asserted grief or the neglect of the resort to the ordained process of amendment. Indeed, it is difficult to conceive of any justifiable motive to revolution in a popular representative government, where the whole sovereign power resides in the people themselves, and their constitution and laws are subject to any amelioration suggested by the popular will. Certainly the founders of our government supposed that, in the scheme they matured, they had forever extinguished the right of revolution.

But those I have enumerated are, at least, the conditions to which the leaders of the present rebellion would be bound to submit their action, if they confess a design to overthrow the Union by force; and, confessing that design, they would occupy simply the position of rebels fully aware of the hazards and the penalty of their undertaking, and presumably ready to meet them. In that view they become liable to be treated as traitors, they, their aiders and abettors. They lose all claim to the protection of the laws, and, still more emphatically, to the right to exercise any privilege of national citizenship. They can hold no office, State or Federal, which implies allegiance to the Government; they abjure or renounce all right to give a vote in either State or national affairs where the qualification demands national citizenship; they are enemies, while in arms, to be met in mortal conflict; when subdued, they are culprits, dependent upon the clemency or the justice of the Government.

It was to avoid these conclusions, as I have said, that the authors of this movement have been careful to veil their proceeding under the official proclamation of the right of secession.

They have found it a difficult task to reconcile the impetuous rashness of their career with this theory. Secession, if honestly conceived to be a right, and honestly pursued, would have sought, at least, a preliminary parley in a convention. It would have moved slowly along through all the customary forms of debate. It would have published a manifesto of its motives for the separation, and calmly laid down the law which defined its privilege, and have shown the unanimity of the Southern people in the belief of it. None of these things has it done. The conductors of the proceeding began in a paroxysm of impetuous enthusiasm; asserted their purpose in a general muster of their forces; put every State in arms, and furnished their magazines of war; boasted of their prowess, with threats of seizure of the Capital, and even of invasion and conquest of the North; glorified themselves with the imagination of an unlimited control over the sympathy and interest of foreign Powers, which they confidently contemplated as prompt and irresistible allies. Their language was not only that of arrogant dictation, but of eager and bloody defiance. They rushed forward with a precipitation which seemed, and no doubt was intended, to preclude all reflection or inquiry into the merits of the cause. There was the ominous glimmer of predetermined war in every step that was taken. Their first act was to close the courts against the recovery of debts, which was sufficiently explained, in the sequel, by the confiscation of all moneys due to Northern creditors. The "Charleston Mercury," exulting in the approach of the day for assembling the State Convention, maliciously spoke of secession as "quasi war," which would justify, what, even then, it recommended, the sequestration of all property in the South belonging to Northern citizens. They seized the national forts and arsenals wherever they could lay their hands on them; insulted the nation and disgraced themselves by a contemptible act of contrived treachery in compassing the surrender of the army in Texas by the complicity of its own officers. They wanted money, and they seized the mint at New Orleans; arms, and they seized the manufactory at Harper's Ferry; ships, cannon, and naval stores, and they forcibly took possession of the navy-yard at Gosport, and pounced upon revenue-cutters, private steamers, and merchant-vessels at their moorings; they even exhorted and encouraged officers of the navy, to whom the nation had confided the guardianship of its honor and its flag, to betray that sacred trust, by an act too base to find expression in the vocabulary of execration. All these things were done, for the most part, in the States where they were perpetrated, before they had even laid the flimsy foundation of an ordinance of secession, and done, too, by the orders and assistance of men who have wearied the public ear with the ceaseless vaunt of their chivalry!

Senators and Cabinet Ministers, as well as officers of the army and navy, did not scruple to retain their posts for no other reason than the advantage it gave them in striking a more sure and deadly blow at the heart of the Government which had elevated them to these honors. History, in its most revolting chapters, does not furnish a page of deeper infamy than that engendered by the madness of this wicked zeal to destroy. Perfidy would seem to have risen to the rank of a cardinal virtue: "*Tanta vis morbi, uti tabes, civium animos invaserat!*"

These acts, let me repeat, were chiefly the forerunners of the deed of secession, perpetrated in a time of peace, and whilst the National Government was yet in the hands of the perpetrators, a helpless, compliant, and almost willing accessary to their design; when the small national army and navy were scattered far and wide; when that untrained military power which sleeps in the bosom of the Republic, and which no peril had yet awakened, could not possibly have been arrayed to meet the emergency; when the public mind was palsied by the sudden stupor which this incredible outrage had cast upon it. In these circumstances was the *peaceful* process of secession set on foot, and the deceived masses of the Southern States stimulated into that unnatural frenzy which wildly hurried them into a treason from which retreat soon became impossible.

When this drama of Secession came to the

stage of its formal enactment in the passage of the secession ordinances, it was characterized by frauds only more stupendous than those I have described, because they implicated a greater number of actors and spread over a wider surface.

Whilst some of the States, perhaps a majority of them, were in earnest in their resolve to secede, the most important States were not; and if the people in these had been left to the free expression of their wish they would have refused. The Convention of Virginia had been elected by a vote which was largely against secession, and the Legislature which authorized that Convention had taken care to provide that no ordinance of secession should have any effect unless ratified by a subsequent expression of the popular will in the regular election. When the Convention assembled at Richmond there was a majority of its members opposed to the ordinance. The scenes that were enacted in the sequence of the proceeding by which that majority was reduced to a minority, are only partially known to the country. Whilst the sessions were open to the public observation the majority held its ground, but amidst what perils and appliances every inhabitant of Richmond at that time knows. The best men of the State, and there were many, who had dared to speak in the Convention in favor of the Union, were exposed to the grossest insults from the mob that filled the lobbies, and by whom they were pursued with hootings and threats to their own dwellings. Still, no vote could be got sufficient to carry the ordinance. The Convention then resolved to exclude the public and manage their work in secret session. From that day affairs took a new turn. The community of Richmond was filled with strife. The friends of the Union, both in the Convention and out of it, — a large number of persons, — were plunged into the deepest anxiety and alarm. They felt that the cause was lost, and that the sentiment of the majority of the State would be overruled. Quarrels arose. Ardent and reckless men were distempered with passion. It was no longer safe to discuss the subject of the day in the streets. The hotels were filled with strangers, loud, peremptory, and fierce. A friend of the Union could not mingle in these crowds without certainty of insult, nor even sometimes without danger of personal violence. The recusant members of the Convention were plied with every expedient to enforce their submission. The weak were derided, the timid bullied, the wavering cajoled with false promises and false representations of the state of opinion in the country. Those who could not be reached by these arguments, but who were found pliable to more genial impulses, were assailed by flattery, by the influences of friendship, by the blandishments of the dinner-table, and finally carried away by the wild enthusiasm of midnight revelry. If the Convention had sat in Staunton or Fredericksburg — anywhere but in Richmond — no ordinance of secession would probably have been passed. As it was, it was a work of long and sinister industry to bring it about. It became necessary to fire the people with new and startling sensations, — to craze the public mind with excitement. To this end messages were sent to Charleston to urge the bombardment of Sumter. The fort was accordingly assailed and forced to surrender, notwithstanding an assurance from the commander that he could not hold out three days for want of provisions. The President's proclamation calling out the militia — which was the necessary and expected consequence of this outrage — supplied all the rage that was wanted. The whole South became ablaze. Men lost all self-control, and were ready to obey any order. The vote of the Convention had been canvassed from time to time, during this process of ripening the resolution of members for the act of secession, and it was now found that it might be successfully put. It was taken three days after the surrender of Fort Sumter, and the public were told it was carried by a large majority. Subsequent disclosures show that upwards of fifty of its members stood firm and preserved their equanimity in this great tempest of passion. The scene at the taking of the vote is described by one of its members as the riot of a hospital of lunatics.

The ratification of this act was yet to be gone through, as prescribed by the law, in a vote of the people to be taken in May. That proceeding was substantially ignored in all that followed. An appointment of members to the rebel Congress was immediately made, to represent the State in the Provisional Government then established at Montgomery. The President of the new Confederacy was forthwith invited to send an army into the State; and, accordingly, when the month of May arrived, troops were posted in all those counties where it was supposed any considerable amount of loyalty to the Union existed amongst the people. The day of election appointed for the ratification found this force stationed at the polls, and the refractory people mastered and quelled into silence. Union men were threatened in their lives if they should dare to vote against the ordinance; and an influential leader in the movement, but recently a Senator of the United States, wrote and published a letter hinting to those who might be rash enough to vote against secession, that they must expect to be driven out of the State. Of course, the ratification found no opposition in any doubtful county. I do not say that, in a free vote, it might not have been carried. Harper's Ferry and the Gosport Navy Yard had both, in pursuance of that policy of profitable sensation-making, been seized in the interval after the passage of the ordinance, and the passions of the people had been still more fiercely wrought up to a fury that had banished all hope of reflection; but my object is to show that the whole secession movement was planned and conducted in the spirit of headlong revolution and premeditated war.

In Tennessee the proceeding was even less orderly than in Virginia. In Missouri it was no better. The attempt was made to carry Kentucky and Maryland by the same arts and the same frauds, but utterly failed. Maryland has repudiated secession and its abettors with a persistent and invincible loyalty. Kentucky, under severe trials and in the actual contest of civil war, has bravely and honorably preserved her faith and repelled every assault. Secession has never won an inch of her soil that it did not temporarily win by the sword, and was not again forced to abandon. In not less than seven or eight elections has she declared her unalterable fealty to the Union by overwhelming majorities. There has never been the smallest ground for a pretence of her acceptance of a place in the Southern Confederacy, where, nevertheless, she is feigned to be represented by members in both houses of the rebel Congress, — not one of whom would dare to show himself openly in the district he affects to represent. We are at a loss to imagine any pretext to claim this stanch and loyal State as one in that treasonable fellowship, unless it be that, being the birthplace of their President, it was necessary to claim it for the Confederacy, in order to avoid the awkward predicament of having rewarded, with the highest honor, the man who could, in violation of the most sacred principles of Southern chivalry — certainly that most ostentatiously clamored in the ear of the world, as distinctive of the Southern cause — consent to draw his sword against his own State.

It is not necessary to pursue further the history of these events as they were developed in the first stage of this ferocious assault upon the Union. Those I have brought into view are quite sufficient to afford us an unmistakable index to the purpose and temper of the Southern leaders. They denote rebellion, and nothing but rebellion, against the lawful Government of the United States, — rebellion conceived in the bitterest hostility and perpetrated with immediate recourse to arms. They prove the dissimulation of that official challenge to the world to recognize, in this terrible attack upon the public order, an honest assertion of a constitutional right. They cast an air of shocking mockery over that peevish plaint which came up everywhere, at that day, from the depths of the Secession, — "All we ask is, *Let us alone!*"

The movement was revolution, — an attempt

to break to pieces an existing dynasty by force; and history will so describe it. Let it be measured by the law of Revolution. If the National Government has grievously failed in its duty to any State, afflicting it with an irremediable wrong, let it be so judged and the revolution vindicated. If, on the other hand, the Government of the Union has done them no wrong; if these complaints have grown out of the mere illusion of a heated fancy; still more, if this wild and reckless outrage upon the peace of society has been prompted by the insolence of ambition; and the credulous hosts of the South have been persuaded by fraudulent misrepresentation to lift their hands against the paternal and beneficent Government that has protected them and given them the inappreciable blessings of a grand and powerful republic; and, above all, if the contrivers of this flagitious plot have been pandering to the rival enmity of the great Powers of the earth, to win their aid in this parricidal enterprise, and have sought, by the unutterable baseness of complicity with them, to shear the American people of that strength which has made them and their institutions the refuge of oppressed Freedom throughout the world — then, we say, let them be held to the strict responsibility of that immense crime.

And, again, if there really be any considerable portion of the people of the United States — sufficiently considerable to originate authentic opinion — who believe in the doctrine of secession and are capable of the enormity of this revolt to bring it into exercise, then, also for that reason, let the war go on until every fibre of that pestilent heresy is cut out and forever destroyed in the fire of popular censure, that no germ of it may remain to engender a new growth of disaster and ruin in this beautiful garden of American liberty.

LETTER VIII.

CONSPIRACY.

MARCH, 1864.

I OPEN now a curious chapter in the rebellion, which brings into view facts that have not been noticed as attentively as they deserve. No complete history of this great disturbance can be written without giving them a conspicuous place in the narrative.

The scheme of separating the States was an old design, almost as old, in the meditation of a class of Southern politicians, as the Union itself. I have had occasion, in a previous letter, to show, in a very cursory way, that some leading politicians of the South speculated on such a project upon the election of the first Northern President, the elder Adams. Disunion then was "a speck no larger than a man's hand." The turn of fortune, which gave to the nation a succession of Virginia Presidents for twenty-five years afterwards, temporarily satisfied these malcontents, and allowed them, at least, to tolerate the Union during that happy period of unbroken Southern dominion. But it only threw the policy of separation into abeyance; for as soon as the continuance of that succession was interrupted, by the election of the second Adams, the old grief returned, and disunion once more became a muttered thought. "The speck" began to expand into a lurid cloud, and grew darker and darker until it broke upon the land in this tempest of blood and fire. That it did not sooner come to a crisis is due alone to the supple complacency of the Democratic party. They flattered the lordly ambition of the aristocratic South, courted its favor, obeyed its behests, and found a satisfactory compensation in being permitted to share in the spoils of the victory which their alliance enabled their patrons to win. It has always been a sad and sore fact for an honest lover of his country to contemplate — the successful cajolery with which the South played off that great party of the North, to make it subservient to the selfish and sectional purpose of putting the whole Union at the foot of its slaveholding master. The good and honest men of that party see this now, and acknowledge it with a blush for the dupery to which, in the full career of their success, they unconsciously — we must hope — succumbed. They were never entirely awakened to this delusion until the cannon of Sumter startled them from the tranquil enjoyment of a friendship which they had found, through long years, too prolific in its rewards to allow a question of its sincerity. But the truth is, and these good gentlemen have so found it, the South never had the slightest esteem for its Northern comrades, the least respect for their worth, or the smallest sympathy with their opinions. Nothing is stranger than that long association of the aristocratic with the democratic element of the country — "the cavalier and the mud-sill," to adopt the elegant phrase of Southern speech — pigging it together in the same truckle-bed. I do not wish to disparage the intelligence or the patriotism of the many excellent men who were brought into that equivocal companionship, in which, doubtless, they had persuaded themselves that they could turn it to account for the good of the country; but it must always be hereafter — since the events of 1860 have opened their eyes — a matter of surprise to themselves that they could have endured so long in such a relation, made such sacrifices of personal independence to sustain it, and worked so diligently to build up the power and exalt the pride of the South at the expense of the nation; and, in the end, to find how little respect they had won from their allies, and how little permanent advantage for themselves. Nothing less than an extravagant obliquity of sight or lamentable blindness could have misled a party, so ostentatious in its boast of a distinctive love of the people, to seek or suffer an alliance or fraternity with a school of politicians who never disguised their contempt for the people, who never spoke of the North but in terms of obloquy, and who never, on the national theatre, professed any other policy than that of absolute Southern domination. It is very apparent now that there never was any real democratic sentiment in the old Southern States, and it is a great marvel that the Democratic party should have been so long in finding that out.

Southern feeling on this point is very outspoken, ever since the rebellion has forced it to throw off the disguise under which it so long but so scantly concealed its aversion to its old auxiliaries. I have at hand a few *memorabilia* which show how contemptuously Southern men regarded, and even how bitterly they detested, the allies they once found so convenient to their needs, and whom they only flattered as long as they could make them their tools. When the time arrived at which they could remove the mask and utter their scorn, it was in no stinted tone that they expressed openly the sentiment which had before been breathed only in the confidence of private life. The " Richmond Whig " of the 28th of May, 1861, very early in the rebellion, gives us a sample of this long pent-up but then explosive estimate of the North.

" We " — says this organ of the ruling sentiment of the seat of the Confederate Government — " must bring these enfranchised slaves back to their true condition. They have long very properly looked upon themselves as our social inferiors — as our serfs; their mean, niggardly lives, their low, vulgar, and sordid occupations have ground this conviction into them. But, of a sudden, they have come to imagine that their numerical strength gives them power, and they have burst the bonds of servitude and are running riot with more than the brutal passions of a liberated wild beast. *Their uprising has all the characteristics of a ferocious servile insurrection.* .... We, of the South, sought only to separate our destiny from theirs, content to leave them to pursue their own degraded tastes and vicious appetites, as they might choose. But they will not leave us this privilege. They force us to subdue them or be subdued. They give us no alternative. They have suggested to us the invasion of their territory and the robbery of their banks and jewelry-stores. We may profit by the suggestion as far as *invasion* goes — for that will enable us to restore them to their *normal condition of vassalage, and teach them that cap in hand is the proper attitude of the servant before his master.*" This in May, 1861; when no blow had been struck but that inflicted by their own cannon upon Sumter, no purpose indicated by the North but that of protecting the Government against violence, and the restoration of the country to every right which had been given to it by the Constitution.

This is but a specimen of the peevish and insane malice against the Free States with which an influential class in the South entered into this war. I could multiply examples of the same madness, exhibited in the same circles, from the beginning of the rebellion to the present day; but I shall confine myself to another extract of later date, to which I refer only because it has a special significance to my subject from its having been provoked by a recent offer of friendship from a remnant of the Northern Democracy which, unmoved by the bitter contumely all along heaped upon them, were still willing to bow to the rod lifted for their chastisement, and, with a shameful abnegation of their manhood, to proffer a new submission to their imperious masters. With what utter loathing is that advance repelled, in the following notice of it by the Government organ of the rebel Confederacy in Richmond, " The Enquirer" of March, 1863. It leaves no room to doubt what portion of the North was the particular object of Southern contempt in that sally of vituperation I have quoted above.

" To be plain," says this paper, in commenting upon the suggestions of these complaisant *friends*, " we fear and distrust far more these apparently friendly advances of the Democrats than the open atrocity of the philanthropists of Massachusetts. *That Democratic party always was our worst enemy, and, but for its poisonous embrace, these States would have been free and clear of the unnatural Union twenty years ago.* It is not the Sewards and Sumners, the Black Republicans and Abolitionists who have hurt us. They were right all along; there *was* 'an irrepressible conflict' between two different civilizations. . . . . If we did not discover, as soon as the Abolitionists, this great truth, it was because the Democratic party, neutral as it was in principle, false to both sides, and wholly indifferent to the *morale* of either of the opposing communities, placed itself between, raised the banner of 'spoils'—and we all know the rest. The idea of that odious party coming to life again makes us shiver. Its foul breath is *malaria;* its touch is death."

Let us remark that this diatribe is directed to that branch of the Democratic party which rejoices in the name of Breckinridge. The Breckinridge Democracy, as it is called, ever since they placed him at their head as their leader, are everywhere, with few exceptions, the secessionists of the South and their sympathizers in the North. All other Democracy has proved itself true and loyal. I could not count a half score of those who refused to go with Breckinridge who are not ardent supporters of the Union. There may be such, but I do not meet them. In the main, the country has found no purer patriots, no more earnest and steady friends, no braver or more willing soldiers in this war than the Democracy who recoiled from marching under that Breckinridge banner; whilst under that banner are gathered all the doubtful and all the zealous defenders, pursuers, and apologists of the rebellion. The schism has brought out the sheep from the goats. They are no longer one, and the Democratic party is redeemed, in the good opinion of the country, by this winnowing which has cast all its true patriots into their proper position, and left the false in an array which all men can see and none mistake. Now, looking to this notorious fact, and measuring its import by the estimate which the South makes of all democracy, and especially reflecting upon the universal acceptance of aristocratic rule in the South, what are we to think of the sincerity of that old-time profession of democracy by Breckinridge himself, by Jefferson Davis, by Toombs, and the whole roll of Southern professors of that repudiated and despised creed? Still more, what are we to think of the manhood, the honesty, and the intelligence of that fragment of the same party in the North, and their obsequious truckling to the haughty guides of Southern rebellion who "shiver" at the proffered contact? What is to be seen in this but the basest spirit of self-seeking and longing for the opportunity to make a bargain, in which the only consideration that can be offered is the betrayal of the country?

With this brief glance at the position held by the Democratic party and the power it possessed, in combination with the South, to control the course of political events, I am now prepared to take up the principal topic of this letter, — the conspiracy by which the disruption of the Union was supposed to be secured.

As long as the Southern chiefs were perfectly sure that they could hold the Government by the aid of the Democratic party of the Free States, they were content that things should move along in a peaceful current. But the demonstration made by each returning census, for the last thirty years, of the rapid increase of the vote of the Free States, was, in their apprehension, a portent of evil. They saw in it the swift advance of the day which was to strip them of that monopoly in the administration of the public affairs to which their ambition had been educated, almost into the conception of it as a birthright. Mr. Calhoun had warned them of the coming of that day, and, in great part, devoted his life to the invention of devices to avoid it. To this end, he taught the dogma of the right of the minority to control the majority, even on the broadest questions of national policy, through the intervention of State sovereignty; asserted the right of nullification; preached the doctrine of a perpetual equilibrium in the Government between Free and Slave States altogether irrespective of the growth of free communities and of the inevitable tendency — which our whole history had exemplified — towards the increase of these through the operation of that economic law which has always been driving slavery from North to South. No matter what disparity between the population of Free and Slave States these changes might produce, it was his theory that the equilibrium of political power should be preserved. To secure this, he proposed, amongst other plans, a dual Presidency, somewhat resembling the arrangement of the Consulship, or more after the manner of that of the Tribunes, in the organism of the Roman Republic, — one of his Presidents to wield the Slave power, the other the Free, and each to be armed with a veto upon the legislation of Congress.

The idea which lay at the bottom of these teachings is that which has manifested itself in such virulent and destructive activity at this day, as a principle wholly incompatible with republican government — that human bondage, namely, may rightfully be insisted upon, not as a temporary and accidental encumbrance, which a wise policy may endure and provide for in its transient state, but as a necessary and wholesome incident of social organization, to be maintained, promoted, and perpetuated by Christian statesmanship as an essential ingredient of the body politic, and even — as the later development of the doctrine explains it — as "the corner-stone" of free government. But beyond and above this emanation of a barbaric philosophy, and more captivating to the Southern mind, the sentiment inculcated by this great leader was a jealous vigilance to provide for and secure, under all contingencies, the political ascendency of the South; and that ascendency, through his influence, thus became not only the universal aspiration of the people of the Planting States, but a postulate which they were determined to elevate into a constitutional right. For the maintenance of this right the governing class — often very justly called the

Oligarchy — of these States have alway been ready to dissolve the Union whenever it should become apparent that, in the Union, they must lose their power.

The obvious danger, in their view, was, that when the population of the Free should reach to a preponderating majority over that of the Slave States, the Democratic party would be compelled to succumb to the popular will of the North, and would not hesitate, in that emergency, to abandon their Southern support for richer and more abundant pastures within their own geographical limits; that this party would bid a cheerful adieu to their old employers, as soon as they could find better service, happy to get rid of patrons whose gratitude for sacrifices made and favors bestowed was confined to the simple payment of the wages of the bargain, and never rose to the height of a sentiment of respect. Astute Southern politicians always prophesied this event, and looked without regret to the day when they would be obliged to face its approach and devise measures to guard themselves against its consequences.

The Presidential election of 1856 was full of signs of this long-meditated crisis. It, however, passed over without harm: the allies were yet true, and the election of Mr. Buchanan was a Southern victory. But it soon became apparent that the South could never gain another, — at least without concessions, which, in the Southern philosophy, would be more disagreeable than a defeat. The leading men of the South, in fact, regarded that as the last election that would ever occur under the Constitution and Union; and, from that day, an active conspiracy was contrived and set in motion to accomplish the object which many had long wished and many more had long feared.

I call it a conspiracy because it was the secret plot of influential and managing men to compass a design which was quite impossible of achievement by open and honest appeal to the people. The good sense and natural affection of the Southern masses would have recoiled from a plot for disunion at any time, up to the day of the first act of secession, if they had been openly invoked to such an enterprise. It required both time and skill " to fire the Southern heart and instruct the Southern mind" for this venture. And I think I may add that, even now, after three years of terrible conflict, a large amount of Southern heart remains yet *unfired* to that dread crime, still more of Southern mind — if it dared speak its secret — yet wholly *uninstructed* in the necessity or the right of this desolating revolution.

In the interval between 1856 and 1860, the great problem which engaged the mind of the plotters was, how to frustrate the Democratic party of the North, which had already found a formidable candidate in Mr. Douglas. The difficulty presented by that problem was surmounted in the manner which it is now my purpose to describe.

The chief element of the plot was the necessity of sundering that party by such a blow as should forever separate its Union-supporting section from those who could be persuaded to destroy the Union — a separation which, it was supposed, would finally gravitate into a specific division of the Northern and Southern members. The great and desired effect of this schism would be to nullify the power of the party in the coming election, insure its defeat, and render the election of the Northern candidate a certain result. This was the theory of the movement. It was particularly important that Mr. Douglas should be defeated, but also important that he should be nominated and kept in the field by his friends. The party was quite strong enough to elect its candidate if it should be allowed to unite its vote upon one name. The tactics of the occasion required two candidates. To produce, therefore, an effective and irreconcilable division, it was necessary to introduce some new and repulsive item into the programme of the Democratic policy; something that would be sure to produce an explosion.

The slave question, as usual, furnished the theme for disturbance. The party was already dividing on the doctrine touching the extension of slavery *into the Territories* and the alleged duty of the Government to protect it there. There was much quarrel on this point, and the North was giving some evidence of making a stand against the Southern demand. Mr. Douglas and his friends were very stanch in resistance, and their cause was growing obstinate in the Free States, whilst it had no little amount of support in the others. The leaders of the plot were not altogether sure that they might not lose the hoped-for division of the party, on this point of protection of slavery in the Territories, by some compromise of opinion, of which they had frequent example in previous canvasses: the North might yield something, or a considerable force from the South might fall in, — and so make a strong party again. It became, therefore, necessary to supply a fresh ground of dissension. This was found in a demand for the renewal of the African slave-trade. If the party could be put under the opprobrium of the slightest suspicion of that design, it was manifest that no Free-State Democrat could incur it and live. The party of the North could go very far, as they had heretofore gone, in defending and protecting slavery, but the revival of the slave-trade could not possibly sit upon any Northern stomach. This, then, was the card to be played.

Accordingly, in the years 1858 and 1859, ground was broken in this new campaign. The right and purpose to revive the African slave-trade was broached to the people of the South, with an intrepidity never equalled in the exploits of the boldest demagogues of any country. The press put out its feelers on this point, and orators of note descanted upon it with a startling audacity. In the lead of these was Mr. Yancey, who both wrote and spoke with great effect upon the subject; and the question, thus thrown open to public advocacy, found many champions and more friends. In the summer of 1859 consultations were held at the White Sulphur Springs of Virginia, where several prominent leaders had gathered together to devise plans for giving full significance and currency to the movement. Soon afterwards, the subalterns who were accustomed to light their lanterns from the fire of the greater lights, were put in motion to circulate and extend the new doctrine, and these took their instructions, not only without reluctance, but with that ready consent which, to an observant spectator, was evidence of a preconcerted scheme that only awaited the order of promulgation to become the experimental strategy of a party.

It was remarkable that this assault upon the honor of the South brought none of those indignant protests which we have heard in old time against the enormity of the slave-trade, — the very mention of which was formerly wont to produce a shudder of disgust. Some few old-fashioned people and old-fashioned presses might have uttered a feeble remonstrance, but these were lost or silenced in the indecent license with which the public mind was abused by the shameless defence of the proposition, both in the written and oral discussions of the period. This unchallenged boldness and this singular silence of reproof were most expressive and fearful omens, to any one who could fully interpret their import, of the calamity that was then brooding over the land. It was very strange to see how little these omens were heeded by the Government, still more, how feebly they awakened the attention of the Northern Democracy. Not even at Charleston, where that Democracy was subsequently assembled in Convention, did its representatives give any sign that they truly understood or appreciated the dangers which lay, as in a mine, beneath their feet.

Whilst the Southern public was thus becoming familiarized to this disgraceful scheme by popular harangues, other agencies were at work to further the cause by practical experiment. Southern citizens of note embarked in the trade; ships were fitted out and dispatched to the African coast; and, for the first time in fifty years, the Atlantic shore of the Southern States was polluted by the landing of cargoes of slaves direct from Africa. The trade could scarcely be called clandestine, with so little concealment was it practised. The whole population seemed to be implicated in saving the trangressors from molestation and in aiding the distribution of the cargoes. The victims of this piracy were openly introduced on the plantations, and a general complicity rendered futile the attempts of the Government — very weak and faltering it is true — to recover them.

We can hardly credit this singular change in the *morale* of Southern society when we read the accounts of the day which give us the details of this trade. South Carolina seemed to have gone mad on the subject. Amongst other incidents I find this, as published in the "Cheraw Gazette": A Col. Hunt had advertised, by way of encouraging this laudable spirit of enterprise, a reward, to be given by him, of a silver pitcher for the best specimen of a native African negro, to be produced at an appointed time and place for inspection; and the "Gazette," with something like gleeful satisfaction, informs its readers that two boys were exhibited, to the owner of whom the prize was adjudged. They are described with the tact of a connoisseur, as remarkably healthy and intelligent, — so intelligent that one of them had already learned to say "wo" when he wanted to stop a horse. This whole affair was undoubtedly nothing less than a bravado to express derision and defiance to the Government and to the general sentiment of the Free States, which the recent importations of slaves had offended; and was, in its way, a step towards that hideous rebellion which is now visiting retribution upon the very actors in that scene.

Every one remembers the farce of the prosecution, in the South, of some of the parties engaged in this iniquitous attempt to revive the trade. According to a statement I have seen, from a paper published either in Charleston or Savannah, — I forget which, — some of the persons arrested and waiting in prison for trial were temporarily released on parole, to enable them to attend a political convention some hundred miles off.

When one of these cases came before the court for trial, Judge Magrath, according to the published reports of the day, gave a very encouraging lift to the friends of the trade, by an exposition of the law which, if not ingenious, was at least new, and was certainly a very courageous onset against that once-universal sentiment of the country, which was wont to boast that an American Congress was the first power in the world that had vindicated the honor of humanity by branding the slave-trade as piracy. The import of this judicial exposition, as stated in the Southern papers, was that slaves purchased abroad by a citizen of the United States were property, and were entitled to the same protection " on the high seas " as any other American property. If they were purchased, *bona fide*, in Africa, — not stolen or kidnapped, — the Government had no right to molest the owner, but, on the contrary, was bound to protect him; and that the Act of Congress which declared the trade piracy could not be construed to apply to such an importation; in that application it would be unconstitutional and void.

Upon this decision, I believe, the party accused was acquitted. I regret that I have not recourse to a report of the trial to allow me to speak more precisely of its incidents. But the prominent and most noteworthy feature of the opinion of the court, as given in the current news of the time, was the assertion of a right to the protection of this property " on the high seas."

Not long after this trial, the Charleston Convention assembled, with a full representation of both extremes of the Democratic party. Its ostensible purpose was to nominate a candidate for the Presidency. The use intended to be made of it by the Southern managers of the plot — some of the chief of which were not of the body, but outside members, holding the wires in their hands, watchers and advisers — was to consummate that feat of which I have spoken, — the dismemberment of the party.

Of all the tricks of political legerdemain we have ever seen, this was the most dexterous, — this exploit of cutting a body in two and setting the severed halves into a battle in which both were sure to be demolished. The neatness of the *tour de passe* was not so much in the division — for that had been often performed before — as in the skill with which the fragments were set in mortal array against each other. I will endeavor to point out some salient strokes by which this was accomplished, as I trace them through the published proceedings of the Convention.

When this body assembled in April there was, as I have remarked, a clear majority for Mr. Douglas. He and his friends rested mainly upon the position of the Cincinnati platform of 1856. They had been stationary whilst the tide of Southern sentiment had been sweeping on in the current I have described. The Cincinnati platform maintained Squatter-sovereignty, as it was called,—which was a protest against any intervention of the National Government on the question of slavery: the Government was neither to mar nor make. It is worthy of remark that, in 1856, certain hot-heads of the South, those present in the Convention, insisted upon this non-intervention with all that angry zeal which is characteristic of the fire-eater, threatening to retire from the Convention and to raise the old spectre of secession if it should be refused.

Four years had swept away that humor, and the demand of the same men was now reversed. It was now for extreme intervention, challenged upon pain of immediate rupture, and, as usual, of peremptory resort to the demolition of the Union.

In justice to the general character and composition of the Charleston Convention, it is proper to say, there is no room to doubt that nine out of ten of its members went into it with no other expectation than that of accomplishing a Presidential nomination, and of standing by it, in good faith, throughout the election; that they knew as little as the outside world of the scheme that was hatching. From all the evidence furnished by the history of their proceedings, from what we know of the men, and from what we have seen of the eminent devotion of many of the most conspicuous members to the cause of the country in its recent trials, we must believe that, if any of the large majority of that body had penetrated the real design of which it was attempted to make them the dupes, they would have denounced it with an emphasis that would probably have saved the nation from these three years of bloody feud and all the misery that is yet to follow. This remark is confined to no sectional division of the Convention. There is proof enough to show that, in the Southern delegations, as well as in the Northern, there were numbers of considerate men whose conduct was guided by patriotic views and true devotion to the Union. Unfortunately, the issues of the time were not in their hands. The plot which frustrated their hopes was secret, known to few, and even now imperfectly understood.

I do not mean to say that there were not many members in that Convention who were not fully alive to the mischief which was likely to ensue from the division growing out of the opposition to the principles upon which the nomination of Mr. Douglas was insisted upon. The speeches of the occasion bear witness to a lively apprehension on that score. But I find nothing to indicate even a suspicion of a premeditated design — which was the real object of the conspiracy — *to promote this division* for the purpose of procuring a defeat to the candidates of both sides of the party, and, by that means, to secure the election of the Republican nominee, as the necessary condition of the *casus belli* upon which the rebellion was predicated.

The plan was to drive the friends of Mr. Douglas in the Convention into a separate organization, by the promulgation of a programme of the party policy which should assert principles he could not adopt and which the people of the North and West could never tolerate; and, if that programme was rejected by the Convention, to form a new party upon it. To this end a Committee was appointed to report the platform of the party. By some means, which do not appear, that Committee was composed of a majority in favor of the ultra Southern view. In the main body of the Convention many resolutions were severally offered looking to the construction of the platform; and these were referred, as often as they were presented, to the Committee, either with or without instructions, as the case happened.

The prominent and distinctive question in dispute was The protection of Slavery in the Territories by the intervention of the National Government.

It was manifestly the purpose of certain members of the Convention, aided by outside advisers who were busy in fomenting the discord of the body, to get into the declaration of the duty of protection, a covert recognition of the slave-trade, in accord with the judicial opinion of Judge Magrath. This purpose first appears in the phrase of a resolution offered by a gentleman from Alabama, — "That it is the duty of the Government to afford legal protection to all classes of property, *slave or otherwise*, in the Territories, or *on the High Seas*."

After some delay and amidst much variety of movement, the same idea comes up in the resolution of another member, in which the phrase is significantly altered: "legal" protection is left out; the term "slave" is omitted, and another clause inserted; it reads: "It is the duty of the Government to protect the rights of persons and property *on the High Seas*, in the Territories, or wherever else its constitutional authority extends." Thereupon Gen. Butler, of Massachusetts, — now distinguished in a very different sphere of action, — gives a pertinent hint that this phrase, of protection of property on the seas, might be construed into a design *to reopen the slave-trade*.

The resolution then goes to the Committee. There, it is found that there is a majority of one in its favor. The vote is 17 to 16, — upon which there is much secret rejoicing amongst the conspirators, and stealthy consultation with Mephistopheles behind the screen. After further deliberation, the Committee make up their report, and this article of the programme finally emerges to the view of the Convention in somewhat modified form. It now appears in the resolutions in this language: —

"That it is the duty of the Federal Government, *in all its departments*, to protect the rights of persons and property in the Territories, *and wherever else its constitutional authority extends.*"

The words "on the high seas" are discarded,

and the periphrase retained which legally covers the same proposition. Gen. Butler's hint had manifestly awakened some solicitude, and it was thought necessary not to name the broad ocean, lest members should become alarmed. The mass of the Convention, as well as that of the country at large, was engaged with the question of protection of slavery *in the Territories:* the "wherever else" of the resolution might pass as an expletive, in which the unwary might see no harm, or it covered the District of Columbia and the Forts, and so might escape immediate observation. The masters of the plot were aiming at the possession of a weapon for future use, which, in due time, they could bring into service. They wanted the ratification of the principle affirmed by Judge Magrath; and they got it. If this programme were adopted, what more distinct sanction could be given to the slave-trade? What more certain than the defeat of any Presidential candidate who should stand upon it?

This was now the majority report. There were two minority reports. The larger of the two reaffirmed the Cincinnati platform of 1856, with some additions on other questions of policy. The other was made by Gen. Butler alone, and presented the Cincinnati platform, pure and simple, without any addition.

Upon these several reports a most earnest debate arose. Members grew angry, and it was very evident that the party was broken, and the plot in full career of successful achievement. Strong appeals were addressed to the mischief-making members, prefiguring the result of this quarrel and warning against it. Governor King, of Missouri, declared "that this platform would nominate Mr. Seward [then the presumed candidate of the Republican party] and make him President."

Mr. Paine, of Ohio, "charged them to reflect, to pause in their mad career; to remember in advance what the consequence of a disruption would be, *and they would see how justly the consequences would be laid on the South.*"

To these warnings, and others in the same tone, Mr. Yancey replied, "that the Democratic party must accept defeat with cheerfulness on a principle rather than seek success with its violation." He concluded his speech, says the report, "by eloquently urging the Southern delegates to be true to their constitutional duty, and not to lend themselves to a palpable wrong to obtain a present victory." This "palpable wrong," let it be noted, was nothing more than an adherence to the principles asserted by the Cincinnati Convention of 1856, in which he and several of his comrades threatened secession and disunion if the doctrine he was now repudiating were not adopted.

The great result for which he and others were struggling was the overthrow of the party and the success of the Republican ticket. This feat was now on the eve of accomplishment.

The Convention, soon after this, came to a vote. The majority report was rejected by 165 yeas to 138 nays. Thereupon a great stir arose. The Convention got into the condition of a beehive in commotion. In a little while a series of abdications began, and, before an hour had passed, the greater part of the Southern members had retired in dudgeon. The egg was hatched; the breach was mortal. From that hour the Democratic party was an effete corporation, and the seed of secession was deeply planted in a rank soil, quickly to bourgeon into a Upas-tree of treason and rebellion, and to distil tears and blood over the happiest and most prosperous nation in the world.

How this breach was followed up by the organization of the fragments into separate bodies; by adjournment to Baltimore and Richmond, and subsequent assemblage of both divisions, at the former city, in June; by further abdications there; by continually widening dissension; by nomination of Douglas on one side and Breckinridge on the other; and then, in due course, by signal defeat of both in the election, and consequent accomplishment of the desired success of the Republican party, need not be told. All that has gone into the record of our melancholy history, where it will remain forever to rebuke and frighten wicked ambition in all future time.

I cannot, however, close this narrative without availing myself of a remarkable commentary upon these events, supplied to my hand by the speech of one of the most intelligent actors in the scene, and one of the most acute of its expositors.

On the 23d of June, 1860, when the scattered Convention was again assembled at Baltimore, and the last abdication took place, Pierre Soulé spoke these words: —

"I am not at all discouraged by the emotion

which has been attempted to be created in this body by those who have seceded from it. We, from the furthest South, were prepared. We had heard around us the rumors which were to be initiatory of the acts which you have witnessed this day, and we knew that *the conspiracy, which had been brooding for months past, would break out on this occasion,* and for the purposes which are obvious to every member. Sirs, there are in political life men who were once possessed of popular favor, and who considered that favor as an inalienable property, and who cling to it as something that can no longer be wrested from their hands. . . . . They saw that the popular vote was clearly manifesting to this glorious nation who was to be their next ruler. More than eight or ten months before the Convention assembled the name of that future ruler (Douglas) had been thrown into the canvass and was before the people. Instead of bringing a candidate to oppose him; instead of creating before the people issues upon which the choice of the nation could be enlightened; instead of principles discussed, what have we seen? An unrelenting war against the individual presumed to be the favorite of the nation, — a war waged *by an army of unprincipled and unscrupulous politicians, leagued with a power which could not be exerted on their side without disgracing itself and disgracing the nation.*

"When the Convention assembled at Charleston, the idea had not yet struck their minds that a movement, of the nature of the one which has been effected, could be based upon the doctrines of the distinguished gentleman from Alabama, Mr. Yancey, who has fathered this secession. It was presumed by *those political intriguers outside of the Convention who were manœuvring the measures through, by which the destruction of the Democratic party was to be effected,* — it was presumed by them that it laid in their power, after raising the storm, to manage and guide it. But it will be found, before forty-eight hours have elapsed, that in that storm they are bound eventually to sink and disappear. *For it is idle for Southern men to disguise the true object of that movement: Secession from the Democratic party can be nothing else than the disruption of that party at the very moment when the hopes of the whole nation are hanging on its continuing in power.* Secession is a word intended to conceal another word of more significancy. *If secession was to find an echo amongst the people of this great Confederacy, then no longer could this republic boast that the structure which its fathers created with so much sacrifice and so much toil was a noble experiment.* Secession must beget disunion. Upon what pretence must secession have been predicted? I wish not to do those distinguished gentlemen, who stepped out of this room this morning, the injustice to suppose that they truly parted from you because of your having decided the question of internal organization in a manner that did not agree with their views. They may give this as a pretence. They may use it as a cloak to cover their desertion from the party, — *but the truth cannot be disguised: whether deluded or not, they are tools in the hands of intriguers and their course must necessarily tend to disunion.*"

This is the speech of Mr. Soulé when the Democratic party, having received the first blow of severance at Charleston, had reassembled in divided fragments at Baltimore, and there completed the dismemberment by retirement, from the major body, of the remaining few who had hesitated at Charleston. The contumacious fragment formed a separate organization, adopted the majority resolutions which had been rejected at Charleston, and nominated Mr. Breckinridge, a man of such popularity, especially in the Border States, as, in the estimate of the conspirators, would be certain to draw off a vote large enough to make the division of the party fatal to the success of either candidate. Breckinridge thus became the representative and symbol of the conspiracy, and the Breckinridge Democracy, wherever you find it, North, South, East, or

West, the very bone and sinew of the revolution.

I ask you to review this chain of facts in the light of preparatives to the rebellion.

First. We have seen that extraordinary and sudden zeal of certain leading Southern men to revive the African slave-trade as a topic of discussion.

Second. The bold enterprise of Southern citizens in the actual pursuit of the trade, the successful importation of slaves, and the distribution and concealment of them by the connivance of planters, and even the derisive ostentation with which the trade was confessed and public opinion defied by the more zealous and intemperate of its advocates.

Third. The decision of the South Carolina judge, and the remarkable sympathy of the community with those arraigned, and their immunity from punishment, or even social censure.

Fourth. The covert attempt to affirm the principles of that decision in the Convention.

Fifth. The preordained breach of the party and the retirement of that portion of the Southern members who were afterwards the most earnest and zealous prompters and champions of the rebellion; and,

Last, Their organization of a new party; the nomination of a candidate whose popularity was a sure obstruction to the success of his rival, and a guarantee for the election of the Republican candidate, — in which event the *casus belli* of the projected revolution rested.

When the groundwork of the rebellion was thus laid, every man who was implicated in the plot took his place. The great fact upon which the dissolution was predicated being thus made sure, it was forthwith announced in a thousand bar-rooms, in the resolutions of numerous popular assemblies, in the harangues of countless orators, and in every Southern press under the control of the conspirators, that if the Republican candidate should be elected the South would withdraw from the Union. Thus, months before the suffrages of November were deposited in the ballot-box, the secession of the States — *teterrima causa belli* — was a predestined event.

LETTER IX.

STATE RIGHTS.

JANUARY, 1865.

WHEN this insane quarrel of the South with the North first came to blows, the question between them, as exhibited in the debates of Congress, in the wrangling of the Peace Conference, and in the negotiations of the two parties, was reduced to this single demand on the part of the South: "We insist upon the right to plant slavery, at our pleasure, in all the free territory of the nation." An almost boundless empire of this free soil lay open to settlement between the Ohio and the Pacific Ocean. The South said, "It is our right to set slavery in every acre of it, and we must have that right acknowledged or we shall rend the nation into fragments." The North replied, "Keep what you have within your own confines, but never will we consent to blast that great free empire of the future with the curse of slavery." And thereupon the South drew the sword to assert and maintain that very act of offence and insult to the sense and humanity of the age for which, nearly ninety years before, Virginia arraigned the monarch of England in twenty successive remonstrances; of which all the colonies complained as a grievous wrong, and which Mr. Jefferson introduced into the Declaration of Independence as one of the chief topics to justify the Revolution.

To this point was the whole controversy ostensibly reduced when the South withdrew in dudgeon from further parley. Every other point was accommodated. Congressional interference with slavery in the States — already prohibited, as all parties agreed, by the Constitution — was proffered to be secured against all future hazard by an irrepealable constitutional amendment. The Missouri Compromise line was substantially restored in the arrangement of New Mexico, which opened every foot of territory south of that line to slave settlement. But all this would not do; the unlimited privilege was insisted on. Upon this a large majority of the nation took their stand; and the South withdrew and put itself in battle array to fight for the extension of slavery into free territory.

Four years of war have made great changes in the aims of the first belligerent. The South no longer fights for the extension of slavery. "We are fighting for our territory," says Mr. Jefferson Davis in one of his late messages to his Congress; as if he wished to impress the outside world, as well as his comrades, with a pathetic sense of the sacred character of his cause. He would have the world believe that this ruthless and despotic Government of the United States has wantonly forced this war upon the South to despoil its people of their country, their homes, and their firesides; and, indeed, it would seem that he had given this idea some currency on the other side of the Atlantic, when English statesmen declared our resistance to the rebellion to be only a contest for empire.

It was a shrewd device on the part of the South to persuade its own people that this war was got up to defend their right to their own soil. Nothing, perhaps, but the end to which this war is hastening will dispel that delusion. Victory for the Union will find every foot of territory just where it was before the strife began. Some owners may have fled from their possessions,—that will be as they have chosen;

many will have perished, and all who survive may find much difference in the value of what is left; but the law of the soil will be the same, the home and country the same, and our renovated nation will move onward in its grand career, the same beneficent protective power which it was before wicked ambition essayed to strike it out of existence. Still, it is true, the great mass of those who have enlisted under the banner of this revolt do really believe that from the first they have been fighting for their own homes. Even so considerate a man as General Lee, the commander-in-chief of the rebel forces, has said that he only took up arms to defend his own State of Virginia against unlawful invasion. Now, let any man tell us what rights of home or country were ever endangered in any State of this Union by the Government of the United States, until the revolting States themselves put them in jeopardy? You say you are fighting for your territory. If you are, is it not because your rash resort to unprovoked war has compelled us — the people of the United States — to fight for *ours!* Were we not, most reluctantly, compelled to fight for a whole section of our country which you were striving to wrench from us? — for our territory of Florida and our territory of Louisiana, both of which we bought with ready money, paid in good red gold? Are we not fighting for our navy-yard at Pensacola, built by the nation, not for the convenience of the State of Florida only, but for the refuge and repair of our shipping, which, from all quarters, plies in the Gulf? Are we not fighting for our forts, all the way from Sumter to the Rio Grande, which we had constructed at great cost, to protect our commerce from injury and insult? Are we not fighting for our Mississippi River, that we may hold it freely forever for the benefit of the nation, without toll or tribute, or homage to any power upon earth? Are we not, in fact, fighting for our rights in our State of Virginia, our State of South Carolina, Georgia, and the rest that have assumed, by proclamation and war, to oust us from privileges which belong as much to each of us as to those who seek to exclude us?

Who can tell me why Louisiana is not as much *my* State as it is the State of John Slidell or of Pierre Soulé, — the two Senators who represented it in the Congress of the Union? Mr. Slidell, a native of New York, and who lived there up to a mature manhood, chose to cast his fortunes in the city of New Orleans. He went with the same certainty of an assured welcome that he would have had if he had elected to make his new home in Albany. He was a *citizen of the Union*, and, as such, was entitled to claim all the privileges of a domicil in any State within its circle. His citizenship in Louisiana was as full and as perfect as that in New York.

Mr. Soulé's case had less original strength than his colleague's. He was a Frenchman, and had no foothold, like that of Mr. Slidell, until he gained the privilege of the national citizenship. This, therefore, was his first step, without which he could make no career for himself in any State. With it, all were open to him. He also chose Louisiana as the theatre of his fortune, obtained his naturalization, and from that day found himself in a position to contend for all the honors an American citizen might win in any State of the Union. Here are two men holding high authority in the Government, exercising great influence over the affairs of the nation, and sent into the Senate by the choice of a State to which for a considerable portion of their lives they were absolute strangers, and into whose confines they had, perhaps, never journeyed until years after they had come to man's estate.

Is it not somewhat startling to hear, after reflecting upon such an experience as this, men of calm and honest judgment, and of educated intelligence, maintaining as a sound, or even a plausible theory of this common-sense, practical Government of ours, that a State of the Union may lawfully — I mean without rebellion and revolution — deny to me or any other citizen of the United States, residing outside of its borders, the same right of domicile and domestication, and right to pursue a path of fortune or ambition which has been so freely and prosperously opened to the Senators from Louisiana? Is it not still more strange that those gentlemen themselves should be found in the ranks of those who assert this right of exclusion? The case of Messrs. Slidell and Soulé I cite only as a conspicuous example. Full three fourths of the whole South, bating the eminence of the position, stand in the same category, — that of migrated citizens who change their domicile from one State to another mainly because they are equally citizens of both. This capacity to range over the Union, protected by a shield of universal citizenship, is the most vital principle of our progress; it is scarcely an exaggeration to say it is one of the most precious of our rights. It strikes me as one of the chief obstacles which must ever be presented to the reflection of those rash men who meditate a severance of the Union, that the great majority of the people, as distinguished from the leaders, will never willingly surrender this unstinted citizenship; and that, whenever such a surrender is forced upon them by the passion or the artifice of a revolution, the result will be but temporary, and the desire to regain what is lost a motive to ceaseless agitation. The present rebellion is daily verifying this remark. Every man on the Northern side of the line feels that the pretension of secession is an invasion of his personal right, whilst multitudes on the Southern side cannot comprehend what they are to gain by limiting the area of their privilege as American citizens. That doubt is now gradually breaking upon their minds for solution.

The plea for this limitation or circumscription of citizenship is attempted to be explained in a theory of State Rights, to the examination of which I propose to devote the rest of this letter.

This subject of State Rights has been greatly mystified, in the popular conception of it, by the uses to which it has been put. The rights of the States, as practically demonstrated in the ordinary operations of State government, scarcely excite debate. Nobody denies them. Every one sees in them a healthful and beneficent power which completely satisfies the people. No one has ever thought of disputing the right of the States to make and alter their constitutions in their own way and at their own pleasure. We are accustomed to see them exercise every function of government within their sphere, without the imagination of a possible objection. They make laws, establish judiciaries, define crimes and punishments, erect corporations, levy taxes, construct public works, regulate education, — in short, enact and do everything appertaining to their internal government and domestic welfare, without a comment from any quarter to suggest a doubt of their power. The only condition required of them in this wide sphere of action is, that they shall do nothing which is forbidden by the National Constitution.

These are the undoubted rights of the States, and might be exercised to the end of time without being questioned. The experience of almost a century has afforded the most abundant proof that, in the orderly administration of these powers, they have been found ample to protect the peace and happiness of the people, and to promote their prosperity.

This formula of State rights is intelligible to the plainest understanding. There is no complexity in it, no knotty question to puzzle the politicians; and the great majority of the people of the whole nation would be, if let alone, and I have no doubt are, perfectly satisfied with it, as expressing the limit of State powers.

Still there is, in the common acceptation, something in the very term, State rights, which obscures this plain, practical demonstration of them, by connecting them with a vague imagination of some attribute too subtle for ordinary minds, — some abstract, reserved power, which may be applied, in great emergencies, even to the dissolution of the Government. It is looked upon as a piece of artillery which may be brought out, on occasion, from a secret arsenal, to threaten the nation and put it upon its good behavior. This notion of State rights comes up from a political school which, for nearly half a century, has been indoctrinating the youth of the country, and especially the Southern youth, in its pernicious philosophy, breeding premeditated hostility to the Union. It has at last produced its proper fruit, in identifying itself and its disciples with this great, bloody, futile rebellion, — in the doom of which it will find, also, its proper punishment.

The distinctive doctrine which characterizes the school asserts an original, inherent, inalienable sovereignty in each State of the Union. It affirms the States to be sovereign powers, possessing an absolute right to determine for themselves their relations to each other and to the whole. It maintains that, as an expedient of convenience, these States have created a common agency to transact their common business in reference to matters of general or foreign concern, to which agency they have agreed, by a compact with each other, to commit certain described powers, with a tacit reservation of their right to determine, each State for itself, whether the agency lawfully performs, in any arising case, the duty assigned to it, and, upon an adverse determination of the question, to decline submission, to nullify the proceeding, and even, in the last resort, to retire from the association. This agency is described as the

Federal Government, which is supposed to exist upon no stronger or more durable tenure than may be deduced from this theory of State Rights.

This conception of the character of the Union and of the powers of the Government has been of slow and reluctant growth. It was discussed at the formation of the Constitution, and rejected. It had a party then, and has had, under various conditions, a party ever since; but it never has had the consent of the people, nor a majority of the leading minds of the country in its favor. The most distinguished of its advocates have been quite as distinguished amongst its opponents; and it has been used and disused, approved and rejected by the same persons and parties at different dates, to suit the political emergencies of the day. It claims to have had its most authentic enunciation in the Resolutions of Virginia and Kentucky, in 1798 and 1799, notwithstanding its positive repudiation by the author of the first of these resolutions, Mr. Madison, and its incongruity with the written opinions of the author of the second, Mr. Jefferson. It boasts of its support in the names of Calhoun, McDuffie, and Hamilton, as the doctrine of South Carolina, in 1832, notwithstanding the deliberate, studied, and cogent refutation of it written by one of these statesmen, and published with the hearty concurrence of the other two, in 1821. It has never, indeed, been a widely accepted doctrine, even in the South, until this rebellion found it to be the most convenient and effective lenitive to the conscience of that multitude of men and women who were in search of a pretext for the indulgence of the pride and passion that revelled in the fancy of a Southern dominion. Then, all at once, it became the creed of the party; an article of faith to the insurgents; an article of fashion and badge of gentility to their sympathizing friends outside of the line of fire.

In reflecting upon these two aspects of the theory of State Rights — that plain exposition of them seen in the daily administration of the State governments, and, in contrast with it, this ultra dogma of sovereignty — it is worthy of remark that every State has thriven whilst it confined its ambition to the scope indicated by the first; and that what discord, feud, and damage have marred the prosperity of any section of the Union, or disfigured the annals of any State, have been coincident with political aspirations towards a power to subordinate the National Government to a State supremacy.

The question to which this review of the State Rights theory brings us is one of great interest: Are the States sovereigns, in the sense which claims for them a reserved inherent power to assert, in any event, a supremacy over the National Government? — in fact, are they sovereigns at all?

According to that scientific definition of sovereignty which we generally find in treatises upon national law, those States are not, and never have been, sovereigns. I mean by this to affirm, that, adopting the notion of sovereignty as expounded in the books, — especially in the writings of European jurists, — there is no such attribute of sovereignty in any State of this Union as belongs to an independent nation. Whatever *quantum* of sovereign power exists in the individual States is *derivative* and *secondary*, not original or inherent; it comes from grant or permission of a higher power, and is subject to all the conditions that higher power may have imposed upon it, or may in future impose upon it.

The present thirty-six States have grown up out of thirteen British Colonies and the territory purchased, or otherwise obtained, by the Union since the adoption of the Constitution. It is to the Thirteen Colonies, therefore, that we must look for any germ of sovereignty that may be supposed to reside in the States.

Confessedly the colonies were not sovereign powers. They were corporations, existing by grants from the Crown. They were invested by their charters with a broad privilege of self-government, reaching pretty nearly to all the functions of domestic or municipal polity now exercised by the States. But still they were subjects of the Crown, bound, in many respects, by the laws of Parliament, and liable to the forfeiture of their charters for misconduct. Of course, such organizations could not be said to possess the character of sovereigns, in the sense in which that character is now claimed for the States.

By what action or means, it may then be asked, could these colonies be converted into sovereign States? I answer, amongst other means,—such as the grant of the parent State, or its abandonment of the colony,— such communities may become sovereign authorities *by conquest*. A people may turn upon the power that rules them, engage in a war of revolution, and, if successful, they may acquire territory and independence by right of conquest, and lawfully become absolutely sovereign.

This leads us to inquire, Were the colonies converted into sovereign States by this right of conquest? Let us take a brief glance at the history of their transformation. The breach between the mother country and the colonies grew out of certain acts of Parliament and Executive interferences, which were regarded as infringements of the rights of the people of these communities as English subjects. These grievances were supposed to assail the political rights of the people of all the colonies. There was, therefore, a common cause of complaint. After much remonstrance from the people, speaking through their legislatures, and through city, county, and other popular assemblages, it became apparent that the discontent was leading to the outbreak of a rebellion, and to the probable establishment of an independent government. This state of things naturally brought to the consideration of the people an inquiry into their capability to sustain a contest with the mother country. The purpose of such a contest would be to conquer a right to possess the country and govern it; their only means to do this lay in the combined strength of the people of the colonies, marshalled in armies. The important question, therefore, was, How were these armies to be obtained and supported? The answer came in a universal demand, from one end of the country to the other, for Union. Before anything was attempted, Union was indispensable. "Let the people unite and make common cause," was the cry from New Hampshire to Georgia. "Let us stand by each other, and, if justice be not done to our demands, let us apply our united force to the extinguishment of the British sovereignty here, and the establishment in its place of a sovereignty of our own!" This was the resolve that rang like a trumpet-note through the country.

The great mass of the people of the several colonies had arrived at this determination in 1776. They had been discussing questions of adjustment and redress in Congress for two years before this, in the hope of peaceful settlement with the Crown; but their propositions were rejected, and the Congress of that year took the final and decisive step, called for by the people, of declaring the independence of the colonies, and making a direct appeal to arms to secure it.

This declaration was made " by the representatives," as they describe themselves, " of the United States of America in General Congress assembled," and announces the act to be done " in the name and by the authority of the good people of these colonies."

In this paper they take occasion to announce the principles of human right by which they held themselves justified in the great enterprise they were about to undertake. These principles found but little support in the political philosophy of that age; they were, however, distinctively American, and have, from the date of this declaration, ever been regarded as the true basis of our Government. Amongst other things, they announce that governments are instituted to secure the rights of the people, and derive their just powers only " from the consent of the governed;" and they declare, moreover, " that whenever any form of government becomes destructive of these ends, it is the right of *the people* to alter or to abolish it, and to institute a new government" on such principles as " shall seem most likely to effect their safety and happiness." This summary of rights is followed by a statement of the many acts of usurpation and tyranny, on the part of the Crown, that were deemed sufficient to warrant the attempt at revolution to which this declaration was the prelude; and the document ends with the momentous proclamation, "That these United Colonies are, and of right ought to be, Free and Independent States."

This is all so familiar to an American reader as almost to require an apology for its repetition. But I have found it necessary to recall these passages in order to ask attention to three points presented by them, which I think worthy of notice: —

1. That they affirm the consent of *the people* to be the only legitimate foundation of government, and the only authority competent to alter the form of government; an affirmation which imports simply *that the sovereignty of a nation resides only in the people.*

2. That this Declaration was issued to the world, by the representatives in that Congress, *as the act, and in the name, of* "*the good people of these colonies;*" and,

3. That in proclaiming the colonies thenceforth to be "*free and independent States,*" it does not assume to describe them as *sovereign* States. They were pronounced free and independent of any allegiance or subjection to the

British Crown; but whether they were to be independent sovereignties or integral parts of a future nation rested entirely, according to the principles formally laid down in this same paper, upon the determination of "the good people of these colonies,"—in other words, "upon the consent of the governed," when the time should come to make a government.

Now, this was the starting-point of the new order of things. The war was just begun. What government the United Colonies then had may be described as of the simplest form of revolutionary, Provisional Government, suddenly got up for the emergency, and to be moulded into something better hereafter. The Colonial Assemblies or Conventions sent delegates to a general Congress to consult and to do what they thought best. This Congress was composed of but one House. The administration was carried on by committees. There was neither time nor temper to construct a government. The movement of the Revolution depended solely on the patriotism of the people and the spontaneous or volunteer obedience of the several colonies to the requests of Congress.

The people flew to arms from every town,

village, and hamlet, and repaired to their several camps wherever they were summoned. Virginians, Marylanders, and Pennsylvanians marched to Massachusetts; and in turn, Massachusetts, Vermont, and New Hampshire sent their men to Virginia and Carolina. In action the whole country was one nation, struggling for one object, — the expulsion of the British power from the circle of the " Old Thirteen," and the establishment in place of it of the power of "the good people of these colonies."

The contest lasted seven years. In the end, Britain was beaten, her dominion extinguished, her sovereignty wrested from her and transferred to another hand. To whom was that sovereignty transferred? To those who conquered it. Who were they? Was it Virginia? Was it Massachusetts, New York, Pennsylvania? No; not any one of these, but all together. The sovereignty, then, went to all together, — " to the good people of these colonies" who originated the war, carried it through, and made themselves a nation, with free choice of their own future organization.

No one of the colonies, during all this struggle, singly declared itself independent. No one had the power to maintain such a declaration, if it had been made. No one, consequently, possessed any capability to make itself sovereign. If, therefore, after the declaration of independence, any State or States became vested with any kind of sovereignty, it must have been by the grant, permission, or acquiescence (which is implied consent) of "the good people of these colonies"; and this, of course, repels the idea of original and inherent State sovereignty.

Now, it did occur, pending the war and after the Declaration, that the States did assume to be sovereign. This is a curious passage in our history, which is marked by some striking demonstrations of a mistake made by our ancestors, in their first conception of the character as well as of the necessities of the Union they were about to establish.

The Articles of Confederation were adopted in 1777, but not entirely ratified until 1781. They were the first expression of the idea of government for the Union. They were begun in an effort at government a year before the Declaration of Independence, and at a time when, as Washington remarked, "No sensible man on the continent desired independence;" when all hoped for satisfactory adjustment of differences with the Crown. The first outlines, therefore, made no reference to sovereign States.

Yet it cannot be doubted — for the evidence is clear — that the Congress of '77 and its successors had a large majority whose conception of the new government did not go beyond the imagination of a League of Sovereign States. The Congress that framed and adopted the articles explicitly declared the doctrine of State sovereignty in the second article, in the following terms: "Each State *retains* its sovereignty, freedom, and independence, and every power, jurisdiction, and right which is not, by this Confederation, expressly delegated to the United States in Congress assembled."

It is worthy of note, that, at the date of this act, the States had not come into possession of sovereignty, freedom, or independence; they were all engaged in the war to conquer these privileges, — a war which had only begun. How could any of these States *retain* what none of them had yet obtained? Much more, how could each of them *retain* a sovereignty which not one of them had even pretended before this to assert for itself, and which the people — the proclaimed source of all sovereignty — had not yet even been asked to confer upon them; which, indeed, they had not yet the power to confer upon them?

It was a strange solecism in the political action of that old Congress, this undertaking to distribute sovereignty amongst the States, when they had not yet secured it for themselves! But the act was liable to a still greater objection; for, supposing that the States had conquered their independence, where did the delegates of that Congress, or any subsequent one, get authority to declare a State a sovereign power? They had just proclaimed it to be a fundamental principle — that all lawful government rested solely on the *consent of the people.* Had they the consent of the people to this act? Did they, indeed, ask the consent of the *people* of any one State to authorize them to form the government they were then devising? No, not one. They were not themselves even elected by the people. They held their seats by the selection of their legislatures, not by popular vote. Did they, when their work was done, refer it to *the people* for ratification? No; the utmost that they did was to refer the ratification to the States; and, in fact, the people never did act upon that scheme of the

Confederation at all. Clearly, the whole proceeding must be regarded, when tested by the principles of the Declaration of Independence, as a usurpation on the part of the States. Still, it is true, the people acquiesced. The great business of the time did not admit of nice debates on points of power, and the people had too much respect for the patriots who guided the public counsels to question what they did in their endeavors to establish the nation. And so, we may admit that the Government of the Confederation, during its short existence, did really recognize — with the acquiescence, if not the consent of the people — the theory of the sovereignty of the States. The history of that old Confederation, its hasty birth, its halting and feeble existence, and its early death, afford irresistible evidence of the utter incompetency of that State-rights theory to answer the most ordinary needs of the nation.

The Confederation was finally ratified by the States in 1781. It had been four years under debate. One of the prominent objections made to it, and which longest delayed its acceptance, shows how naturally the sense of the country, when called into action free from the influence of a political theory, turned towards a true perception of the rights that grew out of the contest of the Revolution. The difficulty that stood in the way of the Confederation was a question of territory. Several of the States claimed, under their colonial charter, a width and breadth of boundary which gave them the area of an empire of yet unsettled land. Virginia, especially, held large tracts beyond the Ohio. The smaller States objected to a confederation which acknowledged State sovereignty over this vast, uncultivated domain. They objected that this domain did not *rightfully belong* to the States that claimed it by their charters, but belonged to all the colonies, *as a national possession conquered from the British Crown* by the united arms and common resources of the whole. They contended, in effect, that no one State had gained anything by conquest, and that what was gained was gained by all for the benefit of all. It was only by a promise of judicious compromise with this objection, looking to a future surrender of their claims, that even the States agreed to adopt the Confederation.

And now came the trial of the State-rights theory. The Confederation formed upon it, even before it went into full operation in 1781, had been pronounced a failure. After the peace, in 1783, the failure became every day more manifest. The letters of the statesmen of that time are full of complaints of the utter inefficiency of the system — the League of Sovereign States — to answer the most indispensable demands of government. Congress was continually suggesting expedients of amendment; the States were constantly endeavoring to reconcile the two evidently incompatible ideas of national welfare and State sovereignty by propositions to patch up the one with grudged and stinted concessions from the other. But all would not do. The country was fast "descending," as Washington expressed it, "into the vale of confusion and darkness." There was really but one remedy against this state of things, and that was finally recognized by Congress in 1787, by the resolution to call a Convention to meet in Philadelphia in May of that year, "for the sole and express purpose of revising the Articles of Confederation, and reporting to Congress and the several Legislatures such alterations and provisions therein as shall, when agreed to in Congress and confirmed by the States, render the Federal Constitution adequate to the exigencies of government and the preservation of the Union."

How that Convention dealt with the question of State sovereignty I propose to make the subject of the next Letter.

LETTER X.

STATE SOVEREIGNTY.

February, 1865.

CHRONOLOGICALLY, the State-rights, or State-sovereignty idea, lasted in theory ten years, from 1777 to 1787. Practically, it was a *caput mortuum* from the beginning to the end of its term. During the war the Government got along in spite of the obstructions of the theory, — propelled by the patriotism of the country; after the war it did not get along at all. The public affairs were generally at a dead-lock. The national finances were in inextricable confusion; the public engagements were repudiated; the current debts were unpaid; the national treaties were unfulfilled; the commerce of the country was left without regulation; the States were in a continual quarrel with each other upon the extent of their boundaries and their separate right to territory, which their united arms had won from its former owner;

insurrection was threatened; the Government had no power either to make peace between the disputants, or to protect itself. The States were all sovereigns, and could conduct things according to their own humor.

When the Convention met, there was a party in that body which rather seemed to favor this state of things. The small States were jealous of the large, and this sentiment was reciprocated from the large States, by a disparaging estimate of the value of the small. But the great and wise leaders of the Convention came to their duty with a full appreciation of the importance of the labors before them. They came with an earnest determination to break up the rickety League of 1777, and substitute in its place A NATION. They came resolved to restore that principle of the Declaration of Independence which had, for ten years, been thrown into abeyance, — the practical acknowledgment of the Sovereignty of the People. An objection was made as to the extent of the authority conferred upon the Convention to create a new government. It was said that Congress had only given them power *to revise* and *amend* the old Articles of Confederation. The reply was: We shall *propose* our new government to the people, and, if they ratify it, it will be the act of the sovereign power of the nation, and so of supreme authority. Upon this basis the labors of the Convention were conducted to the end. The result was, the present Constitution was finally ratified by the people of every State assembled in convention.

The key to a true interpretation of the character and power of the National Government, and of the relation of the State governments to it, will be found in that simple principle, so distinctly announced in the Declaration, — the sovereignty of the people of the Union, or, in the language of the paper itself, "of the good people of these colonies."

As my subject now leads me to make some remarks upon this question of sovereignty, I must premonish you that I entirely repudiate and discard that scientific or professional definition of this term, to which I made some allusion in my last Letter, as accepted in trans-Atlantic treatises on national law, and which definition, I think, has been too broadly adopted into our own.

I have never seen it noticed that our distinctively American form of government is founded on a basis which repels the European, or Old-World, idea of sovereignty and allegiance. I am, therefore, perhaps, venturing on an entirely new ground, when I assert that the relations between the State and the people, as created by our scheme of polity, are not to be measured by the rule which determines the character of sovereignty and allegiance, as known to the monarchical forms of society. Sovereignty and allegiance are feudal ideas. They are correlatives, which suppose a chief on one side and a vassal on the other. They describe attributes and duties of *persons*, — the sovereign lord and the liegeman. One owes protection, the other obedience. The liegeman, according to the old feudal custom, came into court and pledged himself, by oath, "to be faithful to the king and his heirs, and truth and faith to bear, of life and limb and terrene honor; and not to know or hear of any ill or damage intended him, without defending him therefrom." This was, in the primitive days of feudalism, the pledge of *allegiance*, when made to the sovereign, — of *fealty*, when made to a superior or lord who himself was a feudatory to the sovereign.

This idea of sovereignty and allegiance became, in process of time, expanded beyond its original narrow feudal limits, and found a place in our national law, as the expression of the relation between the subject or citizen and the State. But it has never lost, in monarchical countries, its personal attribute; it is invariably, in such countries, exhibited as a personal relation. Sovereignty is personated in the king; allegiance is personated in the performance of the duty due from the subject to the king.

It is easy to trace the transition of this idea into the field of the general rights and obligations which the law of nations of the present age has laid down for the government of prince and people, and, more abstractly, for defining the relation between State and citizen. But it will be found that, throughout this transition, the seminal idea is always preserved; there is always present in it some vestige of its original reference to person. The sovereign is an august power visibly represented in the monarch; his person is sacred, his authority paramount, he can neither give it away nor diminish it; by a fiction of law, he never dies; the *man* may abdicate, but the king cannot; his right comes from Heaven; it is inherent and inalienable. The subject is the servant or vassal of this power, and owes to the possessor of it all respect, deference, and veneration. He is guilty, not only of breach of law, but of indecorum and irreverence, when he disobeys his sovereign. And when he rises against him in rebellion, or abets those who do so, he commits *treason*, which he is educated to believe is a species of parricide. These are the traditional ideas which come to us from the other side of the Atlantic, and which have very notably imprinted their character upon our philosophy in defining the relation between the State and the citizen. We have, however, nothing in our system of government, either State or National, which precisely answers to this trans-Atlantic idea of sovereignty and allegiance, notwithstanding our seeming adoption of it in our national jurisprudence. We have no symbolism by which to represent either; no material, visible sovereign; no form for the manifestation of personal allegiance from the subject. There is nothing apparent to exact that reverence of sovereignty or that humility of allegiance which are uppermost in the foreign conception of government. Then, again, we have nothing from which may be inferred an original and inherent right to govern in any State or National organization. We reduce government to a very simple principle, — the will and consent of the people. We have little or no reverence for old forms or old ideas, but brush them away without compunction the moment we find them to be an obstruction. We have but little veneration for those in authority; they are our servants, and we change them when we choose, — perhaps much too often. We invest government with no mystery, but look upon it as a machine of our own making, which we may take apart and put together as often as we may conceive it necessary for its better working. At bottom, our constitutions, one and all, are, in fact, unwritten. Reducing them to their ultimate term, they may be expressed in one sentence, — " The Government shall be what the people may, from time to time, ordain it." A convention may come together twice, thrice, a dozen times in a century, in any State, or in behalf of all the States, and adopt a set of fundamental ordinances which shall be good until another convention shall supersede them by a new enactment. That is now recognized law all over the country. These conventions even make new Bills of

Rights, — in other words, new declarations of the inalienable, inviolable, and imprescriptible rights of American citizens, — to hold good until another convocation shall discover a fresh and better assortment of the eternal principles of human freedom!

With these differences of doctrine and practice between us and the Old World, it is very obvious we have no need, and, indeed, no possibility, of retaining the Old-World notions of sovereignty and allegiance. We have kept the terms, — and that is all. Sovereignty, in our practical exposition of it, simply means the power to make and execute the laws, and implies, of course, the power to appoint agents to perform this function. That power resides only in the body of the people. The people appoint representatives to organize a government; which government is required and contrived to discharge such duties as the people have agreed to consign to it.

In accordance with this scheme, the people of the United States have ordained, by the Constitution, that the National Government shall exercise, in their name, certain sovereign powers, and shall, within the prescribed limits, also represent their sovereignty. So far, the

National Government may be called sovereign. The same people have also ordained that the States shall, in like manner, be authorized to exercise certain sovereign powers. There were thirteen States, which, as colonies of the British Crown, had been invested with a power to govern themselves according to their own will, within a defined sphere of action. The people, speaking through the Constitution they had made, said to these thirteen States: "You shall exercise all the functions of sovereignty to which you have been accustomed, except in such matters as we find it convenient to prohibit. And, as we propose hereafter to create many more States, we shall give to them the same powers that are allowed to you, subject them to the same restrictions, and make them, in all respects, your equals; that is to say, we shall confer upon them precisely the same amount of sovereignty that you possess."

Now, whatever sovereignty may be said to reside in the States has this origin. It comes *by grant* from the people of the United States; it was not preëxistent, independent, or original. It is a qualified, conditional sovereignty, which, in the European sense, is no sovereignty at all, and which, in our American sense, is the only kind of sovereignty that can exist in any State organism. The sovereignty is in the people, and not in the organized government: *there*, it is a representation, only, of sovereignty. The question then arises, Is there not a separate sovereignty *in the people* of each State? That question I have answered in the last Letter, — " No ; for the people of no State," as I have said, " ever proclaimed or conquered a separate sovereignty." The National Constitution absolutely negatives the claim to original or independent sovereignty in any State of the Union. That Constitution was constructed on the assumption, in which the whole country acquiesced, that a majority of the people of the United States, virtually represented in convention and supported, in a subsequent vote, by a majority of the people of the States, had full authority to propose, ordain, and establish the fundamental law for the government of the whole nation, calling themselves, in the document, " We, the people of the United States."

These concurrent majorities — the great law-originating power of the Union, the universally admitted representative of the national sovereignty — spoke in the language of command and prohibition. They said to each

State, "You must be careful to establish and maintain republican government within your confines; you shall grant no title of nobility. If you fail to observe this law, the nation will interpose and legislate for you. You shall not coin money, nor emit bills of credit, nor collect duties on imports." The phrase was peremptory: "No State shall" do any of those things which the people then thought it expedient to prohibit.

Here is the exercise of a power above all the States. Who was it said, "No State shall do this or do that?" First, the representatives of the people of the whole Union, and, after them, the representatives of the people of the several States, by whose fiat this became law. "We, the people," said it. Could not the same authority have circumscribed State action within still narrower limits? Yes; and they did so. They said: "You shall not make war nor peace, nor treaties, nor have an army or navy without the permission of the nation. You shall not have a post-office, nor a custom-house." In fact, they cut off from the States, one by one, almost every power or attribute which the world is accustomed to regard as a badge or sign of sovereignty, and left them in possession of little more than that municipal power which the world is equally accustomed to regard as the characteristic limit of subordinate governments. It is obvious, then, that the States had a master. How does this agree with the theory of original, inherent sovereignty?

Still, it is true that the States exercise sovereign powers: that is, they make and execute laws. To do this is one of the highest acts of sovereignty. But note, that it is one thing to *exercise* sovereign powers and another to *be* sovereign. The City Council makes and executes laws within its little circle of government, and so far represents a fraction of the great sovereignty of the nation. Yet it is not a sovereign, except on a small scale, in that only sense in which we may call a State a sovereign of larger dimensions. There is really no more inherent and primitive sovereignty in one than in the other. In regard to both State and City Council, — and going still higher, to the National Government, — all these organisms are but *representatives* of sovereign power; the actual sovereignty being resident only in the aggregate people, who can make and unmake each and all of them at their pleasure.

So, whatever sovereignty there is, comes by permission or appointment of the people, and must conform itself to the conditions of that permission.

This is the limit and scope of State Sovereignty, and, whilst it is preserved within this limit and faithfully administered by loyal States, it will be found to be all the State Sovereignty that is necessary to render American liberty forever secure against disastrous assault. Indeed, I can conceive nothing more certain, in the long run, to break down democratic government and overthrow public liberty, than the permanent incorporation of this idea of original, inherent sovereignty into any section, subdivision or fragment of the nation, or anywhere but in the aggregate of the people.

As the fact of sovereignty, according to our republican system of government, is exhibited in the making and executing of the laws, so our allegiance, which is its correlative, consists in nothing more nor less than in faithful *obedience* to the laws. A citizen has no higher duty — I mean no compulsory higher duty — than that. Every man who honestly and truly obeys the laws does all that our scheme of government demands of him in the way of allegiance.

When a Virginia Senator, just at the date of the breaking out of this rebellion, said, on the floor of the Senate, "I owe no allegiance to the United States; my only allegiance is due to the State of Virginia, and what I give to the Government I give through her," he but uttered the words of that sad delusion which has spread mourning and sorrow around every fireside in his native State. If he really meant what these words would seem to imply, it was that he owed no obedience to the laws of the United States, except so far as Virginia permitted him to obey them; and that his State had the right, in the exercise of her sovereign will, to discharge him from the obligation of obeying these laws.

What foundation is there for this vainglorious boast, "I owe no allegiance to the Government of the United States?"

Does not that Government rightfully make laws for the whole nation? Are not these laws "the supreme law of the land?" What title above this — nay, as high as this — has any State to command obedience to its laws, in opposition to those of the nation? The "land" is the whole country, in contradistinction to a State, and embraces the whole round of States.

"The supreme law of the land" is, by its very terms, as it is by its nature, the law of the only sovereign; for there cannot be two grades of sovereigns. The people of "the land" are, *individually*, the subjects of that law and owe it obedience. *Collectively*, they are the makers of that law, and may alter and amend it to suit their own wants. Their *obedience* to this law is the only *allegiance* possible to them. Their sovereign possesses no personality or visible existence to whom an act of homage, allegiance, or fealty can be offered. The sovereign to them is an abstraction, and exists simply in the *law* which rules over all. *Allegiance* is nothing else than *Obedience* to that law.

The same kind of allegiance, and no other, we owe to the laws of the State in which we live. For the State derives its right to make laws to bind those who live in it from precisely the same source as the National Government, — that is to say, the people of the United States. They have agreed that the people of New York and of Virginia may exercise the law-making power within certain limitations; outside of these limitations, they have said New York, and Virginia and the rest shall not make laws. They have said, for example,

"Within the sphere of your domestic affairs, you may make laws, — taking care, however, that, within that sphere, you make no *ex-post-facto* law, nor make any law impairing the obligation of contracts; for these things we forbid. Outside of your domestic affairs, we deny you all power of legislation — except that, if there be anything we have not specifically forbidden you to do, *that* you may do, until we otherwise order. Let the champions of State sovereignty rack their brains over this point as long as they may, they will find no escape from this conclusion — that the people of the United States, as an aggregate political body, are the masters of the whole system of government, both National and State, and lawfully may, and always will, distribute power and arrange the functions of both National and State organizations to suit their own views of the growth and necessities of the nation. Now, whatever State Sovereignty is compatible with that general mastership of the people, the States possess, and nothing more.

It is impossible, it strikes me, notwithstanding all that is said to excite jealousy and distrust of this popular power of the nation, to conceive a safer or more wholesome depositary of the sovereignty of the Union than this. It can have no motive to aggrandize one portion of the system under its control at the expense of another. There is no natural antagonism between the National and State organizations, but, on the contrary, mutual and incessant dependence. There is no necessary conflict of interest; wherever that has appeared, it has arisen out of an assumption, on the part of the States, of prerogatives that were not in harmony with the common welfare. Every man of the Nation is also a man of a State; and it is the aggregate of the men of the nation who form and construct both. It would seem that nothing could be devised so likely to keep both in harmony. Certainly nothing, one would think, would be so certain to render perfect harmony in the Union hopeless, as the independent sovereignty which is claimed in opposition to this theory.

If these views of the sovereignty of the people, as demonstrated in the Constitution, need further development, we shall see them more clearly announced in the provisions made for amendment.

The power to amend, to alter or modify, is a power to construct and establish. I know of no limitation to this power. Has any one ever thought of raising the question of its scope and extent? Would it not be regarded as a very absurd objection to a proposed amendment, that the people of the United States had no right to make it? I take it, that whatever amendment is adopted in accordance with the provisions laid down in the Constitution for making amendments, becomes at once the supreme law. This power may change, one by one, or all together, every feature of the Constitution. It may build States into empires, or dwarf them into municipalities; define State rights, abolish slavery, regulate suffrage, silence the logic of secession, and dispose of the thousand questions that touch the public welfare, with the full authority of a sovereign mandate. The power is unbounded. The only, but the all-sufficient, checks upon it are the responsibility of the representative to his constituents, and the vote of the nation in the act of ratification.

This power to amend, therefore, may be said to exhibit the highest manifestation of the popular sovereignty.

Now, let us see where it is lodged.

We shall find that the Constitution so arranges the process of amendment that every proposition shall come from a majority of the people of the United States, speaking through the representatives of the whole Union ; and shall be ratified by a still larger majority of the people, speaking through their representatives in the several States.

1. The proposition must be made with the consent of two thirds of both Houses of Congress; those in the House representing two thirds of the people of the whole Union ; those in the Senate representing two thirds of the Senatorial constituency, which may or may not be, according to the nature of the division, the expression of two thirds of the States ; for Senators of the same State, by dividing, may neutralize the vote of the State. To this mode of originating an amendment there is an alternative provision. Two thirds of the States may, by their Legislatures, require Congress to call a National Convention to propose amendments. This convention is a single body elected by the qualified voters of the whole Union, and is, in the strictest sense, a representation of the whole people.

2. When the amendment is thus proposed and sanctioned by the people, in either of the

orms of proceeding above described, it is then to be submitted to a second ordeal of popular consent, by its reference to the Legislatures of the several States ; or, if Congress should have reason to believe that State Conventions, expressly elected by the people of each State, would more accurately represent the popular opinion, the Constitution gives it power to order such Conventions to be held and the question of the amendment to be consigned to them. In whichever of these two forms the amendment is submitted for ratification, it requires that the people of three fourths of the States shall thus give their consent to make it a law. When that majority is obtained, then the act is complete, and thenceforth the Government moves in accordance with this new command.

In this process of amendment, it is to be noted that the alteration in the Constitution can only be proposed by the representatives of the nation, assembled either in Congress or in special National Convention ; that it is the people of the United States, represented *per capita*, from equal districts over the whole nation, who possess this great sovereign prerogative of initiating a new arrangement or alteration of the fundamental law; that the supreme law is in the keeping of the Union, and that the Union is the nation. When the amendment is thus initiated, I wish it also to be noted, that it is the people of the States who are called upon to express, through their Legislatures, or — if these be not deemed by Congress reliable exponents of the popular opinion — through State Conventions, their consent to the amendment, by the concurrence of the majority of the voters of not less than three fourths of the States.

This is the machinery provided, by the founders of the Government, for the exhibition of that sovereign power which may make and unmake every fundamental law for the guidance and control of every National and State institution within the Union. When that power once issues its mandate, who can lawfully disobey it? Suppose it were to say that no slavery shall henceforth exist within the confines of the Union; would this command be disputed by any State in the circle? If it should, would the courts uphold it in such dispute? These questions are easily answered. They are answered already. The whole people understand them. The war has made them very intelligible. The great majority of the people of the United States have said, "We must be done with slavery." How have they set about to make that saying good? They propose an amendment of the Constitution. Is there any inherent sovereignty in any State of this Union which can say, I will disobey that law?

It is a subject of curious interest, at this time, to look back to the Convention of 1787 and collect from the proceedings of that body the notions which its leading men entertained of their own power, in conjunction with that of the people, to regulate and establish the whole scheme of the Union. There were some of these men disposed to break up the State system. General Hamilton thought the States ought to be reduced to mere political divisions. Some even thought that the State lines might be altered so as to equalize their several territories. Randolph, Madison, and others were very emphatic in demanding a National Government. Patrick Henry would not accept a seat, to which he had been appointed, because he feared a National Government as hostile to liberty, — a sentiment which he lived to retract. Some were vehement in insisting upon a perpetual license to the importation of African slaves, whilst Mason, of Virginia, denounced not only the trade in slaves, but slavery itself, as a heinous national sin.

What I specially note, as pertinent to my subject, in these incidents, is, that on all sides it seemed to be conceded that, whatever might be the result of their work, — whether it should ultimately limit or enlarge State authority; whether it should establish a nation or a league; consolidate power or distribute it, — whatever might be done, the product would be an entirely lawful achievement, and, when ratified, would be the supreme law of the land to which all must yield obedience. There is everywhere apparent in these proceedings, the conviction that the Convention acted with implicit faith in the sovereignty of the people, as the fountain of all power, and as altogether sufficient to ordain and establish the law which was to regulate both the National and State governments.

There was one question raised in these debates, which was very significant in reference to this subject of State Sovereignty, and which is noteworthy now from the singular misconception to which it has been exposed.

Mr. Randolph, at an early day of the session, offered fifteen resolutions, of which the sixth proposed to confer upon the National Government a power " to call forth the force of the Union against any member of the Union failing to fulfil its duty." Mr. Patterson, also, at a later period, offered a proposition, that "*if any State*, or any body of men in any State, shall oppose or prevent the carrying into execution such acts or treaties, the Federal Executive shall be authorized to call forth the power of the confederated States, or so much thereof as may be necessary to compel an obedience to such acts," &c. These propositions met a prompt dissent from Hamilton, Madison, Mason, and others. They argued against the propriety or expediency of incorporating into the Constitution the idea of, what they called, *coercing a State.*

Hamilton said: " How can this force be exerted on the States? It is impossible. It amounts to *war between the parties.* Foreign powers will interpose, confusion will increase, and a dissolution of the Union will ensue."

He regarded the making of war on a State as an acknowledgment of it as a belligerent, which would allow it to claim the right to form foreign alliances. This acknowledgment, he also perceived, would create confusion in the relations of the people to the Government, as it would enable the State to assume upon itself the responsibility of the citizen's disobedience to the national law; and, what is still more worthy of note at this time, he saw in this admission of a *belligerent* right — what we may now consider prophetic — imminent danger to the Union.

Madison argued to the same effect. Speaking of the predominant theory of the Constitution as then proposed, "he called," says the report, "for a single instance in which the General Government was not to operate on the people *individually*. The practicability of making laws," he added, "with coercive sanctions for the States, *as political bodies*, has been exploded on all hands."

Mason, in a previous stage of the debate, as we read in the notes of the Convention, "argued very cogently, that punishment could not, in the nature of things, be executed on the States collectively, and, *therefore, such a government was necessary as could directly operate on individuals*, and would punish those only whose guilt required it."

It is strange that these opinions of Hamilton, Madison, and Mason should be quoted for the double purpose, First, of showing that they treated the State as a sovereign power; and Second, that, being sovereign, it was their opinion that it could not, *for that reason*, be coerced, or — as the term was used to signify — be subjected to military attack and punishment by the Government. Their argument was the very reverse of this. It said: "Do not recognize, in the constitution you are constructing, any such character in a State as might authorize the National Government to make war upon it, as a sovereign power; if you do so, it will follow that the State may assert the right of a lawful belligerent; shield its citizens from their responsibility to you, by claiming their allegiance to itself; and taking advantage of the war, as putting an end to all treaties and compacts, seize the opportunity to retire from the Union. To obviate such a mischievous relation between the States and the Union, be careful to avoid any recognition of a State as a subject of national hostility, and construct such a government as shall have power — in the language of Mason — 'to operate directly on individuals, and to punish those only whose guilt required it.'

Hamilton, Madison, and Mason evidently thought there should be no more recognition of a power or a necessity to *coerce a State* than to coerce a county or a city. That, on the occurrence of a rebellion, it should be the province of the Government to act only against those, *individually*, who might be resisting, or aiding others in resisting, the due and orderly execution of the laws, and by no means to allow any delinquent to shield himself from punishment by pleading that it was his duty to obey the laws of his State in preference to those of the nation."

It seems almost incredible that any one should argue that a State could not lawfully be coerced *because it is a sovereign power*. The logical conclusion runs in the opposite direction. The only sound reason that could be given for arraying an army against *a State* would be, that the State *was* a sovereign, and entitled to be dealt with as only sovereign powers are dealt with, when argument fails to persuade; for, it is only sovereign States with which nations are accustomed to make war. When States not sovereign transgress, redress is sought, not in war with the subordinate authority, but in the punishment of the individual who obeys its behests to the detriment of the nation.

If the several States were what this ultra State-rights doctrine asserts, sovereign communities, in the sense claimed for them, we have abundant reason, in the dreadful teachings of the last four years, to say that, but for the signal and total prostration of that theory in the catastrophe of the rebellion, the members of this Union would have been destined to quick disintegration and perpetual war. The resistance against this idea of coercion, therefore, by the great leaders of the Convention, supplies another proof, if more proof were wanting, of their wise refusal to assign to the States any higher attribute of sovereignty than that qualified and restricted sovereignty which I have endeavored to describe in this Letter.

LETTER XI.

PEACE.

July, 1865.

I WRITE a short Letter by way of conclusion. The great events which followed so rapidly upon the date of my last, have brought the task I have undertaken to an end. The collapse of the rebellion, in the surrender of its armies and the submission of its leaders, leaves me but little motive to prolong the discussions presented in these Letters.

It was my purpose to say something on that long-vexed question of Slavery, which has so earnestly and so diversely stirred the feelings of both North and South. But the interest in that topic is suddenly and most happily sunk in the fate of the rebellion. Slavery has performed its mission in the world, and is soon to be reckoned amongst the spent forces that have disturbed or assisted the progress of civilization. It is about to pass, with all its imputed merits and demerits, with its wrongs, its crimes, its false pretences, its transient service and whatever modicum of good of which it was capable, into the great storehouse of things finished upon earth, and to be henceforth committed to the accusing record of history.

I regret to find that we have already begun to wrangle about the final disposition of the *débris* which the demolition of that institution has left in the political field. We are troubling ourselves with vain disputes touching equality of races, distinctions of complexion, and settlement of suffrage. The Providence that has conducted slavery up to the day of its extinction, I think, we may safely trust with the final adjustment of the consequences. To me, it seems to be a corollary from the great fiat of that Extinction, that the emancipated slave shall rise, in proper and due progress of elevation, from his debasement, up to the enjoyment of every faculty and every right he may prove himself able to exercise; and that the only impediment which may retard that progress will be found in the attempt to coerce or direct it, by the interposition of the power of the National government. Nothing, it strikes me, can be more appropriate, more certain, or better adapted to insure the success of his advancement, than the authority that belongs to, and is especially cherished by, the State governments, for the regulation of their domestic policy. Let them pursue their own course, and I predict that not another decade will elapse before every State in the Union will find themselves compelled, by the strongest inducements that govern human policy, to use all the means at their command to make the negro a useful and contented citizen.

I do not propose to give my reasons here for this prophecy, but I will merely invite your reflection to the fact, that four millions of people are now added to a scarcely equal number of population who heretofore dominated in the South; and that the aggregate eight millions are hereafter to constitute the body politic of the same region. Does our past experience show that republican government is possible, with one half of the people permanently deprived by the other half of equal political privileges? Reflect upon this question, and call to your aid the history of the progress of political power and especially of the right of suffrage, as these have been developed in our growth, and I think you will find no hesitation in making an answer. Again, I would suggest for your meditation, an inquiry into the character of this emancipated population, and ask you to notice that very prominent fact which every Southern man understands, — namely, that the negro is by nature the most amiable, imitative, and pliable of all human beings; and that, with kind treatment and friendly training, he may be made the most effective and ever ready ally, in all political enterprise, of that class of society which, in his state of slavery, exercised mastership over him. In the consideration of these qualities of this docile race, and these opportunities and inducements to create an influence over it, we may ground our belief in the certainty of the result I have predicted.

And, lastly, I invite you to weigh the value of this remark, — that when the Southern representation in the National Legislature is doubled, (as it will be by the access of this population,) it is against every theory sustained by our political experience, to assume that the nation will not demand the most complete equality of political right for that mass which confers this additional power, and claim for itself the benefit of the kindly sentiment and loyal attachment to the Union, which the conferring of this boon must inspire in the enfranchised population to whom it is given. The gratitude and fidelity of these people, thus earned by the government, the loyal citizens of every State will insist upon being brought to the support of the country, through the instrumentality of the vote.

Referring to the obvious considerations which these views suggest, and which I offer without further discussion, I would, if I had any influence with Southern statesmen, advise them, of their own motion, to take time by the forelock, and provide in their several Constitutions that every colored man who had the qualification of residence, and who had attained to an intellectual culture that enabled him to read his Bible, should be invested with the right of suffrage. Such a provision would disarm all serious opposition to the prompt restoration of the States, lately in rebellion, to all their former privileges, and would disband the political parties which have attempted an organization to confer this right upon the lately liberated slaves.

Touching this question of Restoration, it is pleasant to note how effectively that charitable purpose is already aided by the prompt support of the many old friends in the South we have known in the past, whose stanch loyalty, though long repressed, has never been extinguished in the dreadful trials of the time. I have never abated my confidence in their coming to the post of duty when the day of their service should arrive. They have come forth at the appointed time, and are fulfilling the predictions we have made for them. But we have to rejoice, also, that another auxiliary has come with them into this field of duty, which the country did not expect, at least so soon. Side by side with the most loyal, and even in eager competition with them, have come many of those who had plunged into the *melée* of civil war and either marshalled its forces in the field or led its counsels in debate. This marvel has appeared in conspicuous activity, as if to contradict the ordinary experience of the world as gathered from all other civil commotions, and to furnish one more to the many incidents that illustrate that anomalous character of our people, which makes them incomprehensible to those who do not live amongst them, and altogether inexplicable in the philosophy of those who measure men and States by the standard of Old-World opinions.

The submission of the South was, to the country, a sudden and most happy surprise. It has been too prompt and too general to allow any one to doubt its sincerity. Whether under the influence of a mistaken estimate of political right, or of the illusion of some great wrong and the consequent duty of resistance, or whether impelled by thoughtless passion, or swayed by the mere contagion of a popular frenzy, the men of the South have fought for their cause, and their whole population have endured its privations and its pains, with a bravery and a heroism, of which, in spite of our anger and the sacrifices they have forced upon us, we are secretly and personally proud, as brothers of the same lineage and citizens of the same country. It will hereafter be a point of doubtful determination in the judgment of history, which is most worthy of admiration in this war, — the eager, and, shall I not say, the graceful submission of the conquered, as exhibited in the frank confessions of the host that are now appealing to the President for amnesty, or the extraordinary clemency of the Government in dealing with its erring children.

I notice these characteristics of the ending of the strife, as signs of a happy future, and as persuasions, to both sides, in favor of perseverance in that auspicious course of conciliation and wise submission which will most certainly bring the occurrence, the achievements, and the results of this gigantic conflict of opinion and arms to be accounted, in our future history, as the great purifier and renovator of our Republican Empire, and as the notation of the beginning of a national strength and influence, both at home and abroad, which no people have ever before attained.

At this point I finish my allotted work. If these Letters possess any interest to commend their perusal, I shall be most happy to learn that they have found a special facility of access to those calmer minds in the South, whom the engrossments of the rebellion and the exasperation of conflict have not so seriously disturbed, as to forbid a sober and honest reconsideration of the few but very important topics I have brought into review as the sources of that terrible conflict from which the country has just emerged.